An 1860 English-Hopi Vocabulary
Written in the Deseret Alphabet

An 1860 English-Hopi Vocabulary
Written in the Deseret Alphabet

Kenneth R. Beesley

Dirk Elzinga

The University of Utah Press

Salt Lake City

The Defiance House Man colophon is a registered trademark of the University of Utah Press. It is based on a 4-foot-tall Ancient Puebloan pictograph (Late PIII) near Glen Canyon, Utah.

Library of Congress Control Number: 2015937635

CIP Data on file with the Library of Congress

Contents

Figures

Tables

Acknowledgments

The 1860 English-Hopi vocabulary is reproduced by the kind permission of the Church Copyrights and Permissions Office, the Church of Jesus Christ of Latter-day Saints. It is in the collection of the Church History Library, sometimes abbreviated here as the CHL. We wish to thank the CHL staff, and especially archivists Ronald G. Watt, W. Randall Dixon, and Christy Best, who first allowed one of the authors to examine the then-unidentified and uncatalogued "Indian vocabulary" on December 30, 2002. Thanks are also due to LaJean Carruth and to Amy Carruth, an alert CHL volunteer at that time, who brought the existence of the manuscript to our attention. In July 2011, the vocabulary was cataloged as MS 2977.

We are indebted to Darrell Poleviyaoma from the Hopi village of Musangnuvi; to Bertram Tsavadawa from Orayvi; to Joseph and Janice Day of the Tsakurshovi Trading Post; to Phillip and Judy Tuwaletstiwa; to Kenneth C. Hill of the University of Arizona, editor in chief of the Hopi Dictionary Project; to David Leedom Shaul of the University of Wyoming; to Jonathan and Marcia Ekstrom of the Wycliffe Bible Translators; to Peter M. Whiteley, curator of North American Ethnology at the American Museum of Natural History; and to Charles S. Peterson, a historian of the early Mormon missions to the Hopi, who shared his files and was generous with his time and hospitality. We have also benefited greatly from discussions and shared research with Todd M. Compton, author of a new biography of Jacob Hamblin. Any errors are our own.

We are also grateful to John D. Thiesen, archivist and codirector of libraries at the Mennonite Library and Archives, Bethel College, who generously provided scans of early vocabularies, dictionaries, and linguistic descriptions of Hopi by the Mennonite missionaries H. R. Voth, Cornelius J. Frey, and Jacob B. Epp. These men worked in the Third-Mesa Hopi village of Orayvi in the late-nineteenth and early-twentieth centuries.

Finally, we are grateful to Thales Haskell Smith, a great-grandson of Thales Hastings Haskell, and to descendants of Marion Jackson Shelton—great-granddaughters Billie J. Peterson, now deceased, and Bonnie Clark, and great-great-grandson Bill Shelton—for their help and encouragement.

An 1860 English-Hopi Vocabulary

Written in the Deseret Alphabet

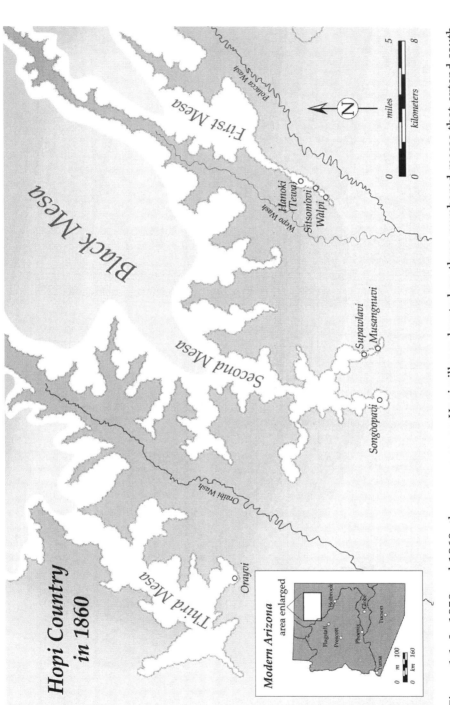

Figure 1.1. In 1859 and 1860, there were seven Hopi villages located on three numbered mesas that extend south from the Black Mesa in what is now northeastern Arizona. Map by Scott Jaquith Art and Design.

CHAPTER 1

Introduction

1.1. The 1859–60 Mormon Mission to the Hopi

In the autumn of 1859, at the direction of Brigham Young, president of the Church of Jesus Christ of Latter-day Saints (LDS Church, Mormon),[1] Jacob Hamblin led a party of seven missionaries—Marion Jackson Shelton, Thales Hastings Haskell, James Pearce, Benjamin Knell, John W. Young, Taylor Crosby, and himself—from Santa Clara and other Mormon settlements in what is now southwestern Utah, to the Hopi villages in what is now northeastern Arizona.[2] Hamblin left two of the missionaries, Shelton and Haskell, in the Third-Mesa village of Orayvi.[3] This book tells the story of this mission and examines new evidence, in particular a recently identified English-Hopi vocabulary of almost five hundred words, that the primary goals of this mission were linguistic, and that Shelton was selected personally by Brigham Young to learn the Hopi language and devise a writing system (what linguists call an *orthography*) for the Hopi language with an ultimate view to translating the Book of Mormon into Hopi and converting the Hopi to Mormonism.

This mission, from October 1859 to March 1860, and henceforth called the 1859–60 mission, was actually the second Mormon mission to the Hopi. The first mission was conducted in the autumn

Figure 1.2. President Brigham Young, circa 1863. Used by permission, Utah State Historical Society, all rights reserved.

of 1858,[4] when Jacob Hamblin led a similar party and left four missionaries—William Hamblin, Andrew Smith Gibbons, Thomas Leavitt, and Benjamin Knell—in what they called the "Moquis" or "Moquitch" village, currently known as Wàlpi and probably also including its overflow or suburb village, Sitsom'ovi (Sichomovi), on First Mesa.[5] Jacob Hamblin and the rest of the group returned home starting on November 18 and suffered extreme hardship enroute, although not nearly as much as the four missionaries left in the Moquitch village without provisions or goods to trade for food.[6] They were soon hungry, cold, and reduced to hauling corn and wood

Figure 1.3. Jacob Hamblin was known as the "Apostle to the Indians" and led fifteen missions to the Hopi. Courtesy LDS Church History Library.

from the valley floor up to the mesa top for their hosts, complaining that what little food they were able to obtain was "filthy beyond description." After relocating to Orayvi and finding the situation just as bad, they visited other villages, including Supawlavi (Shipaulovi) and Musangnuvi (Mishongnovi) on Second Mesa and traded all they had to assemble an adequate "outfit" for their trip home.

After less than a month in Hopi country, those four missionaries started back, arriving on December 26, 1858, at Fort Clara, now Santa Clara, Utah. They were in desperate condition after nineteen days of traveling through rugged desert and crossing the Colorado

River in the dead of winter.[7] Everyone in southern Utah would have heard the story of this first mission of 1858 and of how the missionaries suffered and barely survived; it is not surprising to find hints that Hamblin had some difficulty assembling a new party for the second mission in 1859.[8]

The history of the second mission is fairly well known because Thales Haskell's 1859–60 journal has survived,[9] providing a fascinating account of the trip and the time in Hopi country, including descriptions of foods, customs, legends, dances, and ceremonies. From October 4 through December 1859, the journal was written in the Deseret Alphabet, a non-Roman phonemic alphabet then being promoted by the Mormons as a spelling reform for English.[10] Haskell then continued the journal in traditional orthography to March 26, 1860, when he arrived home.[11] At some unknown later date, Haskell himself produced a longhand transcription of the Deseret Alphabet portion into traditional orthography with light editing; that traditional-orthography text was transcribed to a typescript by the Brigham Young University Library in 1943 and was edited and published by Juanita Brooks in 1944. The 1859–60 mission story has also been retold in a popular western magazine.[12]

Jacob Hamblin has rather little to say in his published autobiography about the 1859–60 mission, it being overshadowed by the disastrous third mission of 1860, when eighteen-year-old George A. Smith Jr., son of Mormon apostle George A. Smith, was shot and killed by Navajos.[13] Hamblin states only that he was directed in 1859 by Brigham Young to take Marion Shelton to the Hopi so that he could "learn their language and teach them."[14] Some historians have read the Haskell journal and noted that Shelton tried to teach the Deseret Alphabet to the Hopi, but the Deseret Alphabet is too often misunderstood to be a new language, a "common tongue" that would "bypass translation" or a "universal means of communication."[15] As we shall show, the Deseret Alphabet is not a language or

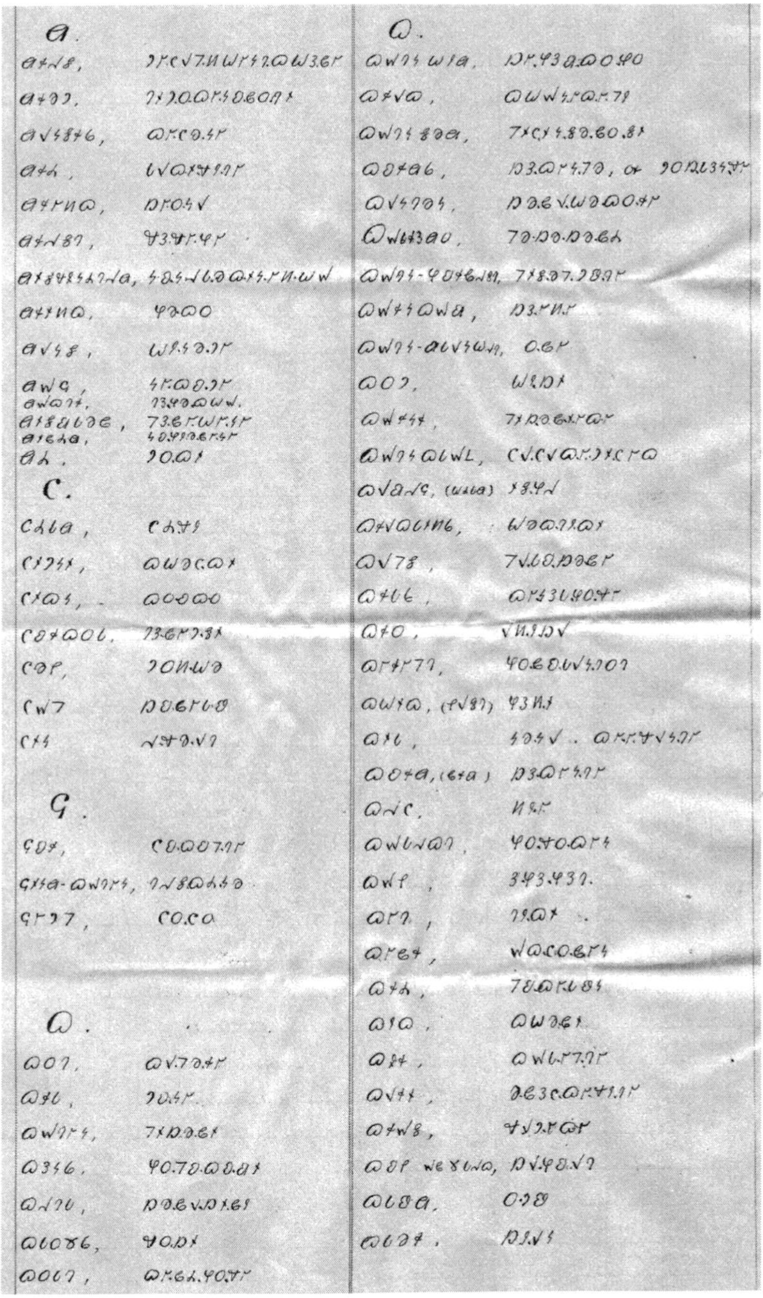

Figure 1.4. A page from the 1860 English-Hopi vocabulary showing entries for D (𐐔), CH (𐐕), J (𐐖), and K (𐐗). Courtesy LDS Church History Library.

a universal means of communication but rather a phonemic alphabet designed primarily for writing English, though it has been used in exceptional cases to write Shoshone, Hopi, Spanish, Asturian, and perhaps also Paiute words.[16]

1.2. An English-Hopi Vocabulary Identified

On December 30, 2002, Kenneth Beesley, one of the authors, was shown an uncatalogued "Indian Vocabulary" in the Church History Library of the LDS Church in Salt Lake City. This vocabulary, written completely in the Deseret Alphabet, lacks a title, author, date, or any other overt identifying information. It is written on six sheets of blue paper, folded to make a gathering of twelve pages and tied with pink ribbons that were probably once red. Each page is about 20 centimeters wide and 32 centimeters tall (8 inches by 12.5 inches) and separated into left and right sides by narrow lines running vertically down the center; each side contains two columns, with easily read English words in the left column matched with words on the right that we have identified as Hopi Third-Mesa dialect (see Figure 1.4).

In this book, we trace the identification and provenance of that vocabulary, setting it in the context of the Deseret Alphabet orthographical reform and the early Mormon missions to North American Indians. In particular, we tell the story of the 1859–60 mission to the Hopi, when Marion Jackson Shelton and Thales Hastings Haskell spent four months in the village of Orayvi, and we present evidence that the vocabulary was compiled by Shelton. The entire vocabulary, comprising 486 entries, is edited and reproduced in this book, showing the original Deseret Alphabet words plus transcriptions into equivalent International Phonetic Alphabet (IPA)[17] and into modern English and Hopi orthography.

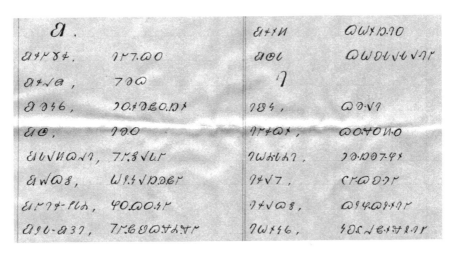

Figure 1.5. A selection from the English-Hopi vocabulary of 1859–60, written completely in the Deseret Alphabet, showing parts of the sections for words starting with 𐐲 (/b/) and 𐑄 (/t/) in English. The first five entries under 𐐲 are 'brother,' /brʌðr/ = /tʌp.ko/ (𐐲𐑉𐐲𐑄 = 𐑄𐑉.𐐿𐐬); 'bread,' /brɛd/ = /pik/ (𐐲𐑉𐑊𐐲 = 𐑄𐐬𐐿); 'beans,' /binz/ = /mo.ri.vo.ʃɪ/ (𐐲𐐬𐑊𐐿 = 𐐬.𐐿𐑄.𐐷.𐐬.𐑄𐑉); 'boy,' /bɔʲ/ = /ti.o/ (𐐲𐐬 = 𐑄𐐬.𐐬); and 'blanket,' /blæŋkɛt/ = /pʌ.sæl.ʌ/ (𐐲𐑊𐐿𐑊𐐬𐑉𐑄 = 𐑄𐑉.𐑅𐑊𐑊.𐑉). These Hopi words are now written, in the de facto standard orthography of the Hopi Dictionary—Hopìikwa Lavàytutuveni, as tupko('at), piiki, morivosi, tiyo, and pösaala, respectively. The gloss for tupko('at) should properly be 'younger brother.' Courtesy LDS Church History Library.

CHAPTER 2

Provenance

2.1. The Deseret Alphabet

2.1.1. Historical Overview

The Deseret Alphabet was promoted by the Church of Jesus Christ of Latter-day Saints, and in particular by President Brigham Young, as a new writing system, what linguists call an orthography, for English. It was designed to replace the traditional English orthography based on Roman letters (see Figure 2.2). Geoffrey Sampson defines an orthography as "a given set of written marks together with a particular set of conventions for their use" for "making examples of a language visible."[1] Peter Daniels and William Bright define writing as "a system of more or less permanent marks used to represent an utterance in such a way that it can be recovered more or less exactly without the intervention of the utterer."[2]

It is important to understand that the Deseret Alphabet was not a different language such as French, Spanish, or German, and not even a consciously invented or "constructed" language like Esperanto, Ido, Klingon or Na'vi;[3] rather, it was just a new orthography, a new alphabet and set of conventions designed primarily for writing and reading English. Because it was a phonemic alphabet, providing one letter to represent each phoneme (each distinctive sound) of English, words were always "spelled by sound," and it was hoped that the Deseret Alphabet would facilitate teaching children how to read and write English.

The Deseret Alphabet first appeared in the winter of 1853–54 and was subsequently used by a few Mormon writers in letters, diaries, meeting minutes, and historical and financial records;[4] it also appeared on an 1860 gold coin and a tombstone, in numerous scripture-based practice articles that appeared in the *Deseret News* from 1859 to 1860 and in 1864, and even in four printed books. *The Deseret First Book* and *The Deseret Second Book*, both published in 1868 with print runs of 10,000 copies each, were readers intended for children.[5] In 1869, the Book of Mormon was published in two versions: the full text,[6] of which only 500 copies were printed, and 8,000 copies of "Part I," which contains roughly the first third of the text and was intended as an advanced reader.[7] The plan was to continue and publish Parts II and III of the Book of Mormon and then to publish the Bible and other Mormon scripture, using proceeds from the sale of the first four books.[8] However, the orthographical reform was unpopular, the books sold poorly, and by 1875, the Deseret Alphabet had clearly been abandoned.[9]

2.1.2. Isaac Pitman's Phonotypy Alphabets

Although notable for its non-Roman glyphs, the Deseret Alphabet was modeled closely on the romanic spelling-reform alphabets being promoted in England by Isaac Pitman (1813–1897) and later in the U.S. by his younger brother and eventual rival, Benn Pitman (1822–1910).[10] Isaac Pitman is today remembered for his system of shorthand, called phonography (sound-writing), for which he was knighted in 1894 by Queen Victoria. Modern versions of Pitman phonography are still in use today. Almost completely forgotten is

THE PHONETIC ALPHABET.

The phonetic letters in the first column are pronounced like the italic letters in the words that follow. The last column contains the names of the letters.

Long Vowels.

Ɛ	ɛ .. *ease*	ɛ
Ħ	a .. *age*	a
Ā	q .. *alms* ...	q
Θ	ɵ .. *awning.* ..	ɵ
Ω	ɷ .. *ope*	ɷ
Ꙍ	ɯ .. *ooze.* ...	ɯ

Short Vowels.

I	i .. *is*	it
E	e .. *egg*	et
A	ɑ .. *am*	at
O	o .. *on*	ot
U	u .. *up* ...	ut
Ꙍ	ɯ .. *sugar* ...	ɯt

Diphthongs.

Ŧ	ɪ .. *ice*	ɪ
Ơ	ɤ .. *oyster* . .	ɤ
Ȣ	ȣ .. *ounce* ...	ȣ
Ꙍ	ɥ .. *use*	ɥ

Coalescents.

Y	y .. *yea*	ya
W	w .. *way.* ...	wa

Breathing.

H	h .. *hay.* ...	haɕ

Explodents.

P	p .. *pole.*	pɛ
B	b .. *bowl* ...	bɛ
T	t .. *toe*	tɛ
D	d .. *doe*	dɛ
Ꞓ	ɕ .. *cheer* ...	ɕa
J	j .. *jeer.*	ja
C	c .. *came* ...	ca
G	g .. *game* ...	ga

Continuants.

F	f .. *fear.*	ef
V	v .. *veer* ...	va
Ꞇ	ŧ .. *thigh* ...	iŧ
Đ	đ .. *thy*	đɛ
S	s .. *seal.*	es
Z	z .. *zeal.*	za
Σ	ʃ .. *shall* . .	iʃ
Ꝥ	ʒ .. *vision* ...	ʒɛ

Liquids.

R	r .. *rare* ...	ur
L	l .. *lull*	el

Nasals.

M	m .. *mum* ...	ɑm
N	n .. *nun.*	en
Ꙧ	ŋ .. *sing.*	iŋ

(') *Vocal*, as in *ab'l, siz'm, hev'n,* &c.

Figure 2.1. The 1847 alphabet of Isaac Pitman and Alexander J. Ellis as it appeared in Pitman's 1850 Bible. This alphabet, obviously based on Roman letters, was the main phonemic model for the Deseret Alphabet. In late 1853, the Board of Regents of the University of Deseret almost adopted a slightly modified form of this alphabet for use by Mormons, but they were persuaded, at the very last moment, to change to non-Roman glyphs.

Deseret	IPA	Deseret	IPA
Long Vowels		*Explodents*	
𐐆	i	𐐙	p
𐐄	e	𐐙	b
𐐆	ɑ	𐐛	t
𐐄	ɔ	𐐔	d
O	o	Ϲ	tʃ
𐐄	u	Ϭ	dʒ
		𐐊	k
Short Vowels		𐐊	g
†	ɪ	*Continuants*	
⌐	ɛ	ρ	f
⌐	æ	Ϭ	v
⌐	ɒ	L	θ
⌐	ʌ	ɣ	ð
٩	ʊ	⸹	s
		6	z
Diphthongs		Ɩ)	ʃ
♩	aʲ	S	ʒ
⊖	ɔʲ	*Liquids*	
ℰ	aʷ	⊹	r
ʔ	ʲu	⌊	l
Coalescents			
⑽	w	*Nasals*	
ⵁ	j	Ɔ	m
Breathing		ɻ	n
ʕ	h	И	ŋ

Figure 2.2. The Deseret Alphabet of 1859–60 had an inventory of forty letters, each one representing a phoneme (distinctive sound) of English. This chart shows the contemporary Deseret Alphabet glyphs and the IPA equivalents used to transliterate them. The subsection titles are taken from the charts of the forty-letter 1847 alphabet of Isaac Pitman and Alexander John Ellis, which was a major inspiration for the Deseret Alphabet.

his second movement, which he considered more important than phonography, called phonotypy (sound-printing);[11] it was intended to reform everyday English orthography.[12] Like the Pitman phonotypy alphabets, which evolved through many versions, the Deseret Alphabet was a phonemic alphabet, providing one letter, or a conventional sequence of letters, to represent each phoneme of English.[13]

Before embarking on the Deseret Alphabet experiment, and even before arriving in Utah in July of 1847, the Mormons almost adopted an off-the-shelf Pitman phonotypy alphabet. On April 16, 1847, when the vanguard company of Mormon pioneers was sixty miles west of Winter Quarters (near modern Florence, Nebraska), Brigham Young took the time to write to George D. Watt, a Pitman "reporter" (shorthand writer) then on a mission in Britain. Young directed him to "procure 200 lbs of phonotype ... to print a small book for the benefit of the Saints and cause same to be forwarded to Winter Quarters before navigation closes ... so that we have the type to use next winter."[14] The "phonotype" referred to by Young was the actual lead type used to print texts in Pitman phonotypy. A response from Watt to Dr. Willard Richards, then second counselor to Brigham Young and later also the founding editor of the *Deseret News*, shows clearly that the alphabet version in question was the 1847 alphabet of Isaac Pitman and his then collaborator Alexander John Ellis (see Figure 2.1).[15] While Pitman was notorious for tinkering with his alphabets, some versions lasting no longer than a month, the 1847 alphabet of forty letters stayed stable for several years and was used by Pitman and Ellis to print a newspaper and several books, including Pitman's 1850 phonotypic Bible.[16]

After the first Mormons arrived in Utah, continuing emigration and basic survival put orthographic reform on a back burner for several years, but on March 13, 1850, the University of Deseret, now the University of Utah, was established under a chancellor and board of regents that included many of the leading men of the new society. Actual teaching was delayed for several years, but the regents were given the task of selecting and promoting an orthographical reform for the Utah Territory. During 1853 the regents had weekly meetings and each was assigned to research and present existing orthographies or new orthographies that they invented themselves.[17] The schemes they discussed ranged from shorthand systems to new alphabets to minimal spelling reforms that used only the traditional twenty-six Roman letters with standardized letter sequences called ngraphs.[18] By November 1853, it seems that the Pitman-Ellis 1847 alphabet was again being favored, and the meeting minutes were being delivered by the secretary, George D. Watt, in a longhand (cursively handwritten) version of that phonotypic alphabet.

Brigham Young took a personal interest in the 1853 meetings, attending many and participating actively. On November 22 and 23, he and the regents worked out a slightly modified version of the 1847 alphabet with some of the glyphs modified or switched, but the result was still very Pitmanesque and romanic. For the second time, the Mormons were about to adopt a Pitman-like romanic alphabet.

Then, on November 29, the meeting was attended by Willard Richards, Brigham Young's second counselor, who was gravely ill with dropsy (now known as edema) perhaps due to congestive heart failure. Richards had not attended the previous meetings, but when he saw the proposed romanic alphabet displayed on the wall, he rose up and vigorously opposed it:

> We want a new kind of alphabet, differing from the compound mess of stuff upon that sheet.... Those characters may be employed in improving the English orthography, though at the same time, it is as I have sometimes said, it seems like putting new wine into old bottles.... I am inclined to think when we have reflected longer we shall

still make some advance upon that alphabet, and perhaps throw away all characters that bear much resemblance to the English characters, and introduce an alphabet that is original, so far as we know, an alphabet entirely different from any alphabet in use.[19]

Some counter objections were tentatively raised. It was pointed out that the key committee had been instructed to keep as many of the traditional Roman letters as possible, and that Brigham Young himself had approved the new alphabet and had already discussed ordering two hundred pounds of type for it. Richards then attenuated his criticism a bit but continued,

> What have you gained by the alphabet on that card I ask you[?] Show me one item, can you point out the first advantage that you have gained over the old one?... What have you gained, you have the same old alphabet over again, only a few additional marks, and they only mystify it more, and more.[20]

Richards believed fervently that the old Roman letters—as they were used in traditional English orthography—varied too much in their phonemic values, that no one would ever agree on their fixed use, and that keeping them would just be a hindrance; a successful, lasting reform required starting with a clean slate. He also argued for economy in writing time, paper, and ink. These arguments anticipated those advanced by George Bernard Shaw in the twentieth century to support the creation of another nonromanic alphabet now known as the Shaw or Shavian alphabet.[21]

Brigham Young and the board of regents were persuaded, the board's modified Pitman alphabet was shelved, and the first version of a new non-Roman alphabet was adopted on December 22, 1853, with thirty-eight original glyphs (letter shapes) devised by George

D. Watt and perhaps also by a lesser-known figure, John Vance.[22] The Deseret Alphabet was born.

2.1.3. The 1859–60 Version of the Deseret Alphabet

During its history of about twenty years, the Deseret Alphabet reform waxed and waned in activity and the alphabet itself went through several variations in phonemic inventory, spelling conventions, and glyphs. The version of the alphabet used in the 1860 English-Hopi vocabulary has forty letters in a one-to-one correspondence with the Pitman-Ellis 1847 letters, as shown in Figure 2.2, including the glyphs ⟨, for the /ʲu/ diphthong in *mule*, and ⊕ for the /ɔʲ/ diphthong in *oil*, which were used in 1859 and 1860. Other extant manuscripts using the same forty-letter version of the alphabet include three letters written by Marion Jackson Shelton in November 1859 and the "History of Brigham Young," kept at roughly the same time.[23] In Haskell's mission journal, written in the Deseret Alphabet from October 4 through December 31, 1859, he uses a very similar forty-letter version, but he idiosyncratically substitutes the glyph ⊖ for ⊕. Ledger C, a financial record kept in the Deseret Alphabet from June 1859 to May 1860, uses a thirty-nine-letter version of the alphabet with the same ⟨ glyph for /ʲu/ but the digraph ⨍ for /ɔʲ/.[24] Judging just by its version of the Deseret Alphabet, the English-Hopi vocabulary can be dated to 1859–60, or at least it was written by someone who had learned that version of the alphabet.

2.1.4. The Fate of the Deseret Alphabet

The Deseret Alphabet is remembered today only by a few linguists, historians, and alphabet hobbyists. After the publication of the four books in 1868 and 1869 and the failure of those books to sell, the Deseret Alphabet was finally abandoned in 1875. But this was not the end of Mormon efforts toward orthographical reform. The Board

of Regents of the Deseret University immediately turned its attention back to the Pitman movement, this time deciding to adopt the
romanic phonotypy alphabet of Benn Pitman, who had set up his
own Phonographic Institute in Cincinnati, Ohio, in competition with
his older brother, Isaac.

Apostle Orson Pratt, who had supervised the transcription of the
Deseret Alphabet books, was in Liverpool, England, preparing to
print the Book of Mormon and the Book of Covenants (now known
as the Doctrine and Covenants) in some version of Pitman phonotypy when, on August 29, 1877, Brigham Young died. Pratt was
called home immediately, the printing project was dropped, and the
Mormons never again experimented in orthographical reform.

2.1.5. Deseret Alphabet to IPA Transliteration

To provide a faithful representation of the original Deseret Alphabet
text in the English-Hopi vocabulary, we have adopted a broad phonemic transliteration that uses, as far as possible, a single IPA letter
for each English phoneme (see Figure 2.2).[25] Thus, the affricate letters C and ?, representing the <ch> in *chip* and the <j> in *jump*,
respectively, are transliterated as the rarely used IPA ʧ and ʤ letters,
rather than the sequences tʃ and dʒ, or even the tied forms t͡ʃ and
d͡ʒ. The diphthongs are notated as a combination of a nucleus and
a superscript glide.[26] Where necessary for clarity, we use slashes
to surround phonemic transcription, square brackets for phonetic
transcription, and angle brackets for traditional and linguist-devised
orthographies.

2.2. The Hopi Language Identification

The initial identification of the vocabulary's target language as
Hopi was based on the word *bread*, written as 𐐁𐑉𐐯𐐼 (/brɛd/) and

translated as ꓶꓳꓳ (/pik/).[27] <Piiki> is the traditional paper-thin Hopi bread made from corn, usually blue corn. There are other entries for corn, beans, watermelon, peach, pumpkin, onion, musk melon, gourd, potato, cotton, sunflower, turkey, chicken, rabbit, horse, panther, wildcat, goat, and sheep, all of which are consistent with Hopi culture. Later the gloss for *dancers* was found to be the telltale *kachina* (ꓳꓩꓚꓳꓩꓩ = /katʃinʌ/), and comparison of the rest of the vocabulary with modern Hopi dictionaries quickly confirmed the identification.

2.3. Author Identification

2.3.1. Mormon Missions to the Hopi

The compiler of the English-Hopi vocabulary was the missionary Marion Jackson Shelton (Figure 2.3), who, with his companion Thales Hastings Haskell (Figure 2.4), lived four months in the Third-Mesa Hopi village of Orayvi during the winter of 1859–60.[28] This was the second Mormon mission to the Hopi; from 1858 to 1873, there were no fewer than fifteen Mormon missions to the Hopi, all under the leadership of Jacob Hamblin.[29]

The Mormons, and Brigham Young in particular, were fascinated by reports of these Indians who "cultivated the ground," "owned sheep and cattle, raised grain, and lived in adobe [really stone with mud mortar] houses, some of which are three or four stories high."[30] At this time, the Mormons generally referred to the Hopi as Moquis, Moquees, Moquiches, or Moquitches; these terms were used by the Spanish and the surrounding tribes.[31]

2.3.2. The Second Mormon Mission to the Hopi

After the sobering experience of the first mission of 1858, when the four missionaries lasted less than a month in Hopi country and

Figure 2.3. Marion Jackson Shelton (1833–1886) was personally chosen by Mormon President Brigham Young in 1859 to go to Hopi country, learn the language, and devise an orthography for writing it. During the winter of 1859–60, while living in the Third-Mesa village of Orayvi, he compiled the English-Hopi vocabulary of 486 entries, written completely in the Deseret Alphabet. Photo courtesy of Billie J. Peterson, his great-granddaughter.

barely survived their journey home, better planning and provisioning went into the mission of 1859–60. Brigham Young tried to combine the Hopi missionary work with the Deseret Alphabet movement, which was enjoying a revival after the disruption of the Utah War of 1857–58. The official goals for the missionaries of the second mission were to learn the Hopi language, to devise an orthography based on the Deseret Alphabet, and to teach the Hopi to read and

Figure 2.4. Thales Hastings Haskell (1834–1909), an experienced and trusted missionary under Jacob Hamblin, was asked at the last minute to stay with Marion Shelton in the Hopi village of Orayvi for one year. The two missionaries lasted four months before heading home. Haskell kept his journal of the mission—from October through December 1859—in the Deseret Alphabet. Used by permission, Utah State Historical Society, all rights reserved.

write their own language using that orthography. Young's longer-term goals were to translate the Book of Mormon into Hopi and convert the tribe to Mormonism.

Such a task called for a proven teacher with some linguistic sophistication and experience with Native American culture and languages. The man chosen by Brigham Young was Marion Jackson Shelton, born on August 30, 1833, in Spring Creek, McDonough

County, Illinois. From all evidence, Shelton was a remarkable character and led a most interesting life, but no biography is currently
available. We will sketch his known history here, concentrating on
the events leading up to the mission.[32]

The thirteen-year-old Shelton arrived in the Salt Lake Valley
with his family on July 29, 1847, and made a report, from memory,
listing the members of the entire Pueblo pioneer company.[33] He was
probably on his own at the time of the 1850 census of Salt Lake City,
where he appears as Jackson Shelton, age seventeen. An entry in a
surviving journal, which covers March 1858 to June 1859, places
him at Fort Atkinson, Kansas, on the Arkansas River, in the summer
of 1852, when he was in close contact with a number of Indian
tribes.[34] In an 1859 letter to LDS Church Historian George A. Smith,
Shelton indicates that he spent the summer of 1852 chiefly with
the Comanches and shows a solid understanding of their customs
and history, correctly identifying them as a branch of the Shoshone
tribe; he also stayed a winter with the Cheyennes. He writes of the
"Kiway" (Kiowa), Osage, and especially the Apaches, citing various
bands, including the "Lepan" (Lipan Apaches), and their locations,
and identifies their head chiefs by name.[35]

From 1856 to 1859, Shelton was employed as a schoolteacher
in southern Utah, most notably at the frontier settlement of Fort
Harmony, south of Cedar City, where he taught the children of John
D. Lee,[36] notorious for his part in the Mountain Meadows Massacre
of September 1857.[37] In October of 1857, Shelton was sent by the
church to San Juan Bautista, California, to organize members there
to relocate to Utah during the Utah War. In his journal, written
partly in Pitman shorthand, Shelton makes what appears to be his
first entry in Deseret Alphabet on January 18, 1859, while in Washington, near modern St. George, Utah. It reads simply 𐐊𐐃𐐻 𐐝𐐀𐐬𐑊—
𐐎𐐰𐑊𐑉 𐐼𐑉𐐴 𐐰𐑌𐐼 𐏌𐑊𐐲𐑈𐐲𐑌𐐻: "taught school—weather dry and pleasant."
The letters here and in a few subsequent Deseret Alphabet entries

are thick and clumsy, the work of a beginner. In traditional orthography, Shelton could write a fine hand, and his Pitman shorthand
has been judged simple, but competent and legible, by LaJean Carruth, a Pitman shorthand expert who transcribed the journal.[38]

Shelton was living at Fort Harmony in October 1858 when he
wrote a letter describing the location and customs of the "Cheyennes
and Arrapehoes [*sic*]" based on his experience living among them.[39]
As a result of this report, "Pres. Brigham Young directed Geo. A.
Smith, who directed the southern Utah settlements and the Southern
Indian Mission, to write to J.[*sic*] J. Shelton, and ask if he would like
to take a few brethren and go among the Cheyenne and Arrapahoes
Indians and preach to them."[40] Nothing came of this proposal, but it
shows that Shelton was already noted by church leaders as an expert
on American Indians.

On March 7, 1859, Shelton wrote a letter that includes the first of
several proposals for improving the Deseret Alphabet.[41] The Deseret
Alphabet samples in this letter are still clumsy, and the text indicates that Shelton had already been trying, with some difficulty,
to teach the Deseret Alphabet to the "Lamanites," almost certainly
Paiutes, around Fort Clara. (The Lamanites are a people described in
the Book of Mormon, and Mormons commonly believe that modern
Native Americans are their descendants.)

At Fort Clara in March of 1859, Shelton was also teaching Spanish
classes at night.[42] Later that year, the twenty-six-year-old Shelton
was in Salt Lake City, meeting several times with Brigham Young
and George A. Smith, and was consulted about the Hopi and other
tribes. For some time, he was a clerk in the office of George A.
Smith, who was the church historian. The *Journal History* entry for
June 4, 1859 records that "the president [Brigham Young] asked
Brother Shelton where he had been since 1849. He gave a narration
of his adventures in the Indian Country among the Sioux, Arapahoes,
Apaches, Camaches [*sic*], Kiways, utahs [*sic*], Shoshonies and in

New Mexico, Chichawa, Sonora and California." Unfortunately, the narration of adventures was not recorded. At the same meeting, Young "wished him [Shelton] to take some lessons from [George D.] Watt on the new alphabet," in which Shelton already had some facility, and "Bro. Shelton gave his opinion that the Spanish and most of the indian [sic] languages could be written in the Deseret Character as far as he understood it."

In a report dated simply June 1859, Shelton wrote to Brigham Young, "Having been advised to make my self thoroughly acquainted with the Deseret Alphabet, I submit the following as the result of my studies and researches, for your examination."[43] The report is a surprisingly sophisticated phonotactic analysis of English text written in the Deseret Alphabet, specifying the restrictions on how the letters, representing phonemes, combine into words, with a comparison to the treatment of vowel sounds in "Dr Webster's" dictionary.

Shelton also concluded, quite correctly, that the Deseret Alphabet lacked a letter for the neutral or "obscure" vowel, now known as the schwa, and proposed a way to fix the problem.[44] Isaac Pitman and Alexander J. Ellis were quite aware of the neutral vowel, or vowels, but these were purposely excluded from their 1847 alphabet and other versions as being "not only unnecessary, but highly inexpedient" in "ordinary phonetic printing" and likely to promote "slovenly" pronunciation.[45] The general principle, inherited by the Deseret Alphabet, was that "phonotypic representation should be based on careful and deliberate pronunciations such as might be used in the production of words in isolation."[46]

The talks with church leaders continued. The *Journal History* entry for June 15, 1859, records, "Evening—Geo. A. Smith, Jacob Hamblin and Marion J. Shelton went to the President's office and had conversation with the president about the Moquis Indians, Colerado [sic], etc." These discussions led eventually to a mission call; on September 18, 1859, "Marion J. Shelton was blessed and set apart to go on a mission to the Moquis Indians, by the Twelve [Apostles], John Taylor, mouth."[47] On the same day, Brigham Young wrote this letter to Jacob Hamblin.

Great Salt Lake City Sept 18th 1859.

Elder Jacob Hamblin,

Dear Brother:-

As Bro. Shelton is about leaving for your place, I improve the opportunity of sending a letter of instruction for your guidance. It is my wish that you should take all the articles which were furnished you here to the Moquiches and leave a few brethren in their midst to give them instruction[,] to teach them the use of the utensils sent and otherwise learn them how to labor to advantage[,] also cleanliness in person and cookery, and as soon as they become sufficiently familiar with their language [orthography] present to them the Book of Mormon and instruct them in regard to its history and the first principles of the Gospel. Instil into their minds purity of character and holiness and seek to elevate them above their present low condition.

Bro. Shelton had also better remain as he can instruct them in the new alphabet and perhaps reduce their dialect to a written language which they will soon learn and understand to read and write [emphasis added]. Instruct the brethren to be just and honorable in all of their transactions with them and not permit a spirit of covetousness or speculation to enter into their minds or influence them in any of their acts, but on the contrary. In all of your intercourse with them in every possible way seek to do them good.

May the Lord give you wisdom and aid you and the brethren, who are associated with you in gaining and exercising the salutary influence over the dark and benighted minds of the Lamanites into whose midst we have so providentially been thrown. It is for us to improve the privilege so opportunely given to lead them back to a knowledge of the Lord God of their Fathers.

Your Brother in the Gospel
Brigham Young[48]

This letter is the best evidence to date that Shelton was charged with creating an orthography for the Hopi language (in Young's nineteenth-century terminology, to "reduce their dialect to a written language"), with an ultimate goal of enabling the Hopi to read the Book of Mormon in their own language. It would appear that the letter was hand-carried by Shelton from Salt Lake City to Jacob Hamblin in Fort Clara, triggering the following response:

Ft. Clara Oct 9th 1859.
to Pres. Brigham Young

Dear Bro your leter of instructions by the politeness of Bro Shelton I received the contents of which I rejoiced in as I was geting up the company for that trip to the Moquiches and urgin[g] the nesisity of some of the Bretheren remaining with that People[.] it helpt us out. 7 of the Bretheren started yesterday with impliments for working or[e.] road of[f] over the first mountain 20 miles East of this place which is the most dificult this side of the Colerado.[49]

our company will consist of .11. men .15. pack and riding animals .4. oxen one cart .1. whip saw heavy-sleag [sledge-hammer] fo[r] brakeing rock picks hoes shove[l]s and spaids .75. lbs bredd breddstuf one beef ox to kill at the Colerado and one to leave with the Boys that stay with the Natives and nesesary carpender [carpenter] tools together with the goods you furnished me[.][50] you roat you wanted me to take them to the Moquiches I felt under the greatest obligcions to doe so when I left your office and to make such disposition of them as would gain a salutary influence with them...."[51]

This letter, and Thales Haskell's journal, indicate that Hamblin had some difficulty finding young men willing to join the second Hopi mission and, especially, to agree to stay in Hopi country; they had no doubt heard the story of the missionaries of 1858, who barely survived.[52] Hamblin eventually assembled and led a team of six others—Marion Jackson Shelton, Thales Hastings Haskell, Taylor Crosby, Benjamin Knell, James Pearce, John W. Young—from the frontier settlements around Santa Clara, across the deserts, across the Colorado River and to Hopi country, arriving in the westernmost village of Orayvi on November 10, 1859.[53]

On their arrival, Hamblin still had not decided whom to leave as a companion for Shelton, who was supposed to stay among the Hopi for a whole year. This was not negligence but rather part of Hamblin's modus operandi—he considered himself a visionary man, and he apparently felt that the "Spirit" would best guide him to the proper choice at the last minute: "My mind rested upon Brother Thales Haskell. I went to him and told him that he was the only one I could think of to remain with Brother Shelton, but he had been out so much [on previous Indian missions] that I disliked to mention the subject to him."[54] But Haskell, a loyal and trusted man, who at twenty-five was already a veteran of five years of missionary work on the Indian frontier, knew what was coming: "I told him that I was willing to stay and do the best I could."[55]

Haskell's 1859–60 journal of this mission was originally written in the Deseret Alphabet from October 4 to the end of 1859, when he switched to traditional orthography. When Haskell later transcribed

the Deseret Alphabet portion into traditional orthography, he added
the following editorial comment:

> Such a feeling of utter loneliness I never experienced
> before, for search the wide world over I do not believe
> a more bleak, lonesome, heart sickening place could
> be found on the earth where human beings dwell. And
> here we are, Bro Shelton and me, with strange Indians
> who talk a strange language, situated far from the busy
> haunts of men. Who but Mormons would do it? Who but
> Mormons could do it? Make up their minds to stay here
> a year![56]

In spite of this first impression, and several subsequent bouts of
"the blues," Haskell and Shelton both held up quite well. Though not
without cultural prejudices and complaints about lice and hygiene,
the missionaries were remarkably adaptable, open minded and
impressed. Haskell remarked several times on the honesty of the
Hopi and wrote, "I can truly say that as a general thing this is the
best people I ever saw."[57]

Haskell describes a number of the Hopi dances, and Shelton actually joined them on occasion. They saw kachina "images" and masks
being painted. The cultural curiosity was often mutual: "Had one
fellow who wanted to know if the Mormon women had whiskers
like mine. I politely informed him they had not."[58] The Hopi were
also entertained by Haskell's singing, accompanied by Shelton on
the fiddle.

The missionaries joined in community projects, including the
repair of a kiva, which Haskell called a workshop: "Helped the
Indians repair their workshop. They discovered that I could outlift
any of them so they gave me all the heavy lifting to do and gave me
the interesting name of, Konesoke [honsoki] (bear claws)."[59]

Figure 2.5. The Orayvi village plaza, circa 1896, showing the ladders used to gain access to the roof entrances of ground-level houses. Haskell and Shelton made themselves useful by building several ladders in Orayvi. Copyright The Field Museum, #CSA2342. F. H. Maude.

They also built deadfall traps as part of a communal wolf hunt, tried to build a spinning wheel, and, most astonishingly, were in demand for making ladders. For security, Hopi houses had no doors at ground level and were entered by first climbing a ladder to the roof, and then letting oneself down by another ladder through a hole in the roof. The external ladders could be drawn up to prevent intrusion. The underground kivas were also entered via ladders. The Hopi therefore appreciated ladders and obviously made their own, but the missionaries' novel ladder-making technique, which somehow involved "ripping open" cottonwood poles, perhaps with the rip saw mentioned by Hamblin, or more likely with axes and splitting wedges,[60] attracted great attention and several ladder-

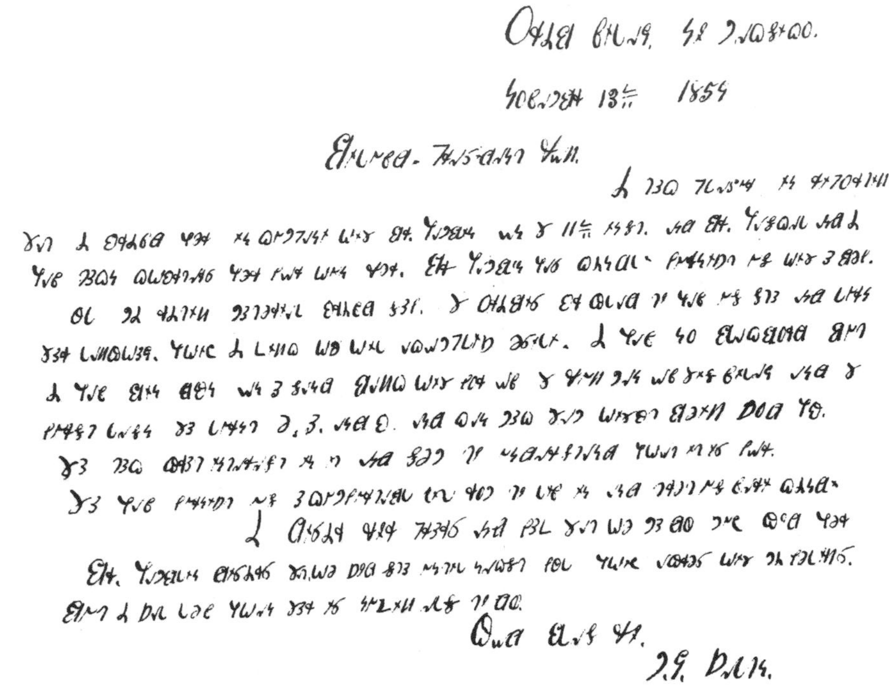

Figure 2.6. Deseret Alphabet letter from Marion J. Shelton to Brigham Young, November 13, 1859, shortly after he and Thales H. Haskell arrived in Orayvi. Courtesy LDS Church History Library.

building commissions in Orayvi.[61] Their fame spread, and the missionaries were soon invited to the village of Songòopavi on Second Mesa especially to make ladders.[62]

Four letters by Shelton are known to survive from this mission, plus a fifth letter, a brief mission report, written shortly after his return. The first three letters were written in the Deseret Alphabet on November 13, 1859, just a few days after his arrival, so that Hamblin could carry them back to the Mormon settlements. One of the letters is addressed to Brigham Young, and shows that Shelton lost no time in starting to teach the Deseret Alphabet to the Orayvis.

Oraibi Village, New Mexico.[63]
November 13th 1859

Beloved President Young,

I take pleasure in reporting
that I arrived here in company with Br. Hamblin on the
11th inst.[64] and Br. Haskell and I have taken quarters
here for one year. Br Hamblin has kindly furnished us
with a beef.

All my writing material arrived safe. The Oraibis are glad
to have us stay and learn their language, which I think
we will accomplish easily. I have no blackboard but I
have been down on a sand bank with four of the young
men of this village and the first lesson they learnt Ə [/i/],
Ɛ [/e/], and ℧ [/ɑ/] and can make them without being
showed how. They take great interest in it and seem to
understand what it is for. They have furnished us a com-
fortable little room to live in and treat us very kindly.

I desire your prayers and feel that we may do much good
here[.] Br. Hamblin desires that we should stay until next
fall which agrees with my feelings. But I shall leave when
there is nothing else to do.

God bless you.

M. J. Shelton[65]

Another letter, addressed to George A. Smith and "others" is a
delightful account of Shelton's first impressions of a Hopi village:

Oraibi Village. New Mexico
Nov. 13. 1859.

Beloved Brothers,

I am sitting on top of my dwelling. The way we get into our house is through a little square hole in the top. We go down a ladder and when we get down we have to stand stooping or bump our heads. Yesterday morning I took breakfast with one of my red friends. I went up into the third story and seated myself on the floor beside my friend. The lady of the house brought a "chahkahpta" [*tsaqapta*], or earthen jar, full of soup, and a basket full of "peek" [*piiki*]. (a bread resembling blue wrapping paper folded) The old lady seated herself, a little boy also and lastly the cat to its place with its head in the soup and its tail on the peek. So we broke peek dipped soup with our fingers and had a merry breakfast.[66]

These Oraibis beat the Mormons for children. a few dogs and cats and horses, a good many sheep, turkeys, and chickens with lots of peaches, corn, beans, melons, and pepper, squashes &c. These things they raise.

Their workshops [kivas] are under ground. Their work is chiefly making blankets and belts of wool—they raise some cotton, and are not addicted to begging, but are very intelligent and industrious indians.

I write jokingly but truefully [*sic*]. But, brothers, I shall see you next fall and will have learned more about these folks by that time and then we'll have big talks together. Yours,

M. J. Shelton.[67]

The third Deseret Alphabet letter, addressed only to George A. Smith, gives an account of the route to Orayvi and ends with the following scene:

> Now for these Oraibis. They are over me and around me looking at me write. They all wear blankets which they make. They are very industrious. Their houses are built of undressed rock and mortar. From one to four stories high. They are very kind to me and "all is Right."[68]

The fourth letter was written on November 16 in traditional orthography to George A. Smith.

Oribe Village, N.M.
Nov. 16th 1859.
G. A. Smith,
Dear Brother,

As br. Hamblin starts for home tomorrow, I embrace the oppertunity [*sic*] of writing a few lines to let you know how we progress.

We arrived here on the 10th inst. I told br. H[amblin]. that this was as far as I wanted to go[69]—he agreed with me and left br. Haskell and I here to prepare winter quarters while he with four men proceeded to the Moqich [*sic*] and Moshamineel villages.[70] He returned yesterday morning with the brethren not having met sucsess [*sic*] in trading and having had some things stollen [*sic*].[71] It appears that the U.S. has been giving those indians spades, hoes, &c, and they think it unnecessary to trade for them.[72] Last night we heard that the troops would be here to day so br. Hamblin started four men with the animals to go on 40 miles, while he remains with us today.[73]

(This is to save the animals in case the troops should come) Br. H. has left br Haskell here in charge of this portion of the mission. I employ my time in studying the language and and [sic–over a page break] in instructing them in the Deseret Alphabet. I find that I acquire the language very readily, and that those who I have gave lessons have taken right hold of the alphabet, and several of them know the six first characters, Ә, З, Ɛ, Ɵ, O, [sic—only five listed, omitting Ꝺ] and we can hear them hollowing the sounds throughout the village[.]

They have some peculiarities in their ~~tounge~~ tongue that I never have heard in any other. You will please tell the president [Brigham Young] that I have had to introduce another character which I sincerely hope will meet his approbation. It is simply this, |, A strait [sic] mark.

There are many things that I could write but it is very unpleasant writing on top of these houses with the sand flying over every thing. Br H[amblin] leaves a lot of things with br. Haskell for him to trade.

These people very much need spinning wheells [sic] and looms. and a small horse mill would be an advantage to them. They lay out a great deal of labor in grinding their corn on a stone. They twist their yarn on a stick in their fingers and weave blankets with a few strings and a stick[.] (You would have to see it to understand it.[)]

These indians are very anxious to have us stay and have furnished us a little house to live in[.] They have stole nothing of us as yet, but they must see every thing[.][74]

If the soldiers come here I expect that they will endeavor to either send or take us away but I am bent on staying untill [sic] my mission is fullfilled [sic] which I think will take till next fall. If they come we have concluded to tell what we are here for and let them rip[.] Give my love to the family and clerks, and oblige me by handing the enclosed as directed with my regards and beleive [*sic*] me

Your Brother
in Christ
M. J. Shelton

I desire your prayers and faith that I may accomplish the will of <u>Him</u> who sent me.

M.J.S.[75]

Though Shelton enthusiastically starting teaching the Deseret Alphabet as soon as he arrived, and Haskell mentions the project a number of times in his journal, a quick descent into disappointment is clear. On November 28, Haskell wrote, "In the evening we spent an hour or 2 with old Thur [*sic* in the Brooks transcription for Kur, short for Kuringwa (Kuyngwu), the acting chief of Orayvi]. He said the Oraibis will never learn to read and write."[76] By the beginning of December, bribes were considered: "This morning we talked of the propriety of giving the Indian who we call Alma something to induce him to learn the deseret alphabet. For from some cause or other he has refused to receive instruction."[77]

In March 1860, not long before the men gave up and went home, teaching efforts were renewed, and the missionaries fashioned some pedagogical aids: "We today cut out some letters of leather to see if we could not learn young Indians their use but it seem[e]d impossible.... Tryed in vain to learn the Indians the misteries of the Deseret Alphabet.... Br Shelton is trying to learn some to write."[78]

On March 23, 1860, on their way back to mission headquarters at Santa Clara, the missionaries met John D. Lee in Washington, Utah. Shelton asked Lee "the favor of staying a few weeks at [Lee's] house at [Fort] Harmony to prepare his Journals for the Press." Permission was granted, and Shelton traveled to Fort Harmony on March 29.[79]

Shelton refers in his letter of November 16 to George A. Smith to the invention of a new letter, a "strait mark," and the text seems to imply that the new character was invented for writing some phoneme of the Hopi language, in which he heard "some peculiarities ... that I never have heard in any other." However, this mark does not appear at all in the English-Hopi vocabulary; rather, Shelton used this straight mark (I) in some English texts to represent the schwa, which had no letter in the standard Deseret Alphabet. The straight mark appears in the following letter, written in the schwa-augmented Deseret Alphabet by Shelton after arriving in Fort Harmony. Here he blames his failure to teach the Deseret Alphabet on the constant dancing or ceremonial obligations of the tribe.

> Harmony, Washington County, U[tah] T[erritory]
> April 3rd, 1860.
>
> Pres. B. Young:
>
> Beloved Brother,
> it is with heart-felt gratitude to my Heavenly Father for his preserving kindness that I now seat myself to inform you that Br. Haskell and myself arrived from our mission to the Moquitch nation on the 24th ult. I have been unwell since my arrival or I would have written sooner.
>
> Knowing that you feel a deep interest in the progress of all that effects [sic] our fellow beings I will say that we far succeeded [sic, for exceeded?] our anticipations in establishing ourselves in the confidence of those to whom we were sent. Their traditions tell them that they have been very numerous but when they should become reduced to a very few, as at present, that a white people should come from the west and teach them to put away

their sins and that they would do so and would become one with that people and a great and mighty people. This tradition, so soon as we were able to talk to them, gave us great influence as they claimed us to be that people which their tradition speaks of.[80]

They are very anxious to have us come and reside with them and teach them. They are also anxious to have wheels and looms introduced among them. They desire that a blacksmith and a carpenter should live with or near them.

Br. Haskell and I explored the surrounding country but could find nor hear of any place nearer than the Colorado for establishing a settlement. About three and a half days from the nation, at or near the mouth of Beaver Creek, (where it empties into the Colorado) on this side of the Colorado) is the only place that we found or heard of that is suitable.[81] At this place there is wood, water and grass and sufficient land for 25 or 30 families. I think that wagons can be taken there without farther [*sic*] difficulty than is consequent to breaking a road. When the road is broken it will probably take seven days from here to the mouth of Beaver. I believe that the Colorado bottoms may be tilled and that they will produce the best of cotton and tobacco. From the impossibility of approaching them from the land they would have to be visited in small boats. As, doubtless, many of them have never been explored by a coyote, much less a Paiute.

As an instance of the influence we gained with that people it is sufficient to say that, without solicitation, they gave us two horses, saddles, bridles, ropes, in fact a complete "traveling outfit." They furnished us provisions to do us home and numbers brought provision to us that we had to refuse in consequence of having all that we could pack. Numbers of them came near shedding tears at our leaving. They were over anxious for us to remain with them, but the spirit dictated otherwise.

I did not succeed in learning them to write as the dancing commenced shortly after our arrival there and continued until we left, but I am satisfied that with proper cards I can learn them to write in one winter more. I have the ice tolerably well broken.[82]

Not wishing to make this communication overly lengthy, as, if providence so directs, I hope to see you ere long. I will subscribe myself

Your brother in the gospel

M. J. Shelton.

(P.S.) *My journal and that portion of the language that I have reduced to writing I will bring with me when I come* [emphasis added].

M.J.S.[83]

What Shelton refers to in the postscript as "that portion of the language that I have reduced to writing" is almost certainly the English-Hopi vocabulary. The journal, which Shelton planned to edit and publish, has unfortunately been lost.

To convey the color of the original letter, the next-to-last paragraph, which starts "I did not succeed," is included here in the original schwa-augmented Deseret Alphabet and an equivalent phonemic IPA transcription (see Figure 2.2).

𐐴 𐐼𐐮𐐼 𐑌𐐱𐐻 𐑅𐐲𐐿𐑅𐐨𐐼 𐐮𐑌 𐑊𐐲𐑉𐑌𐐮𐑍 𐑄𐐯𐑋 𐐻𐐳 𐑉𐐴𐐻 𐐰𐑆 𐑄 𐐼𐐰𐑌𐑅𐐮𐑍 𐐿𐐱𐑋𐐯𐑌𐑅𐐻
𐑇𐐱𐑉𐐻𐑊𐐮 𐐪𐑁𐐻𐐲𐑉 𐐵𐑉 𐐲𐑉𐐴𐑂𐐲𐑊 𐑄𐐩𐑉 𐐰𐑌𐐼 𐐿𐐱𐑌𐐻𐐮𐑌𐐷𐐲𐐼 𐐲𐑌𐐻𐐮𐑊 𐐶𐐨 𐑊𐐯𐑁𐐻. 𐐺𐐲𐐻
𐐴 𐐰𐑋 𐑅𐐰𐐻𐐮𐑅𐑁𐐴𐐼 𐑄𐐰𐐻 𐐶𐐮𐑄 𐐹𐑉𐐱𐐹𐐲𐑉 𐐿𐐪𐑉𐐼𐑆 𐐴 𐐿𐐰𐑌 𐑊𐐲𐑉𐑌 𐑄𐐯𐑋 𐐻𐐳
𐑉𐐴𐐻 𐐮𐑌 𐐶𐐲𐑌 𐐶𐐮𐑌𐐻𐐲𐑉 𐑋𐐬𐑉. 𐐴 𐐸𐐰𐑂 𐑄 𐐴𐑅 𐐻𐐱𐑊𐐲𐑉𐐲𐐺𐑊𐐮 𐐶𐐯𐑊 𐐺𐑉𐐬𐐿𐐲𐑌.

aʲ dɪd nɒt sʌksid ɪn lʌrnɪŋ ðɛm tʊ raʲt æz ð dænsɪŋ kɒmɛnst ʃɒrtlɪ ɑftər aʷr əraʲvəl ðer ænd kɒntɪnjəd ʌntɪl wi lɛft. bʌt aʲ æm sætɪsfaʲd ðæt wɪð prɒpər kɑrdz aʲ kæn lʌrn ðɛm tʊ raʲt ɪn wʌn wɪntər mor. aʲ hæv ð aʲs tɒlərəblɪ wɛl brokən.

In later years, Haskell returned several times to the Hopi, notably for a five-month stay during the winter of 1862–63,[84] and both he and Shelton were reputed in later life to be Hopi speakers. Haskell worked among Native Americans in the Southern Indian Mission for a total of thirty-five years, gaining a lasting reputation as an Indian interpreter, negotiator, and peacemaker. According to a biography written by his grandson Albert E. Smith, Haskell learned to speak an additional four Indian languages plus Spanish,[85] sang well, including songs in Indian languages, wore moccasins all the rest of his life, and was said to "out Indian the red men themselves."[86] Haskell lived a relatively long life, dying on June 13, 1909, and was buried in Manassa, Colorado.

Research continues on Shelton's later life, which is not nearly as well known. After the Hopi mission, he returned to northern Utah, married Emmaline "Emma" Durfey, and had a child, Henry Miller Shelton, in 1861. He was divorced six months later, apparently because Emma did not care for his frequent travels. In the 1860s, he was teaching in Fillmore, Utah, and he wrote a number of reports to Salt Lake, including one on "Moquis" customs and traditions.[87] In 1871, he married Katura Maria Kofford in Heber City and they had two children, born in 1872 and 1873; she died the day after the second child was born. But his travels continued, most notably when he served for a month as "Indian interpreter" to Major John

Wesley Powell during his second Colorado expedition of 1871–72. Shelton later worked as an attorney in the Heber, Utah, area and as a surveyor in Castledale.

The death of Marion Jackson Shelton was a mystery for many years. In 1999, after years of searching, great-great-grandson Bill Shelton finally located his unmarked grave in what had been the paupers' section of the Provo, Utah, cemetery; a family organization took up a collection to buy the stone that marks the grave today. Oral tradition from two branches of the family holds that Shelton was killed by a "drunken Indian." Given that he was only fifty-three and that the death and burial dates are recorded as just October 1886, with no exact day, the suggestion of foul play is all too credible. However, Bill Shelton confided in a personal communication that his latest research reveals that his ancestor died less dramatically from chronic alcoholism.

The judgment of history on the early Mormon missions to the Hopi and other Indian tribes is that they did not achieve their religious goals. Historian Charles Peterson writes that "the Indian mission fell short in its primary purpose of conversion."[88] Non-Mormon historians have come to the same conclusion, but their accounts of overall Hopi-Mormon relations have been generally sympathetic. Harry C. James writes that "the Mormon missionaries were among the very few who entered the Hopi country to win converts who did not resort to cruel coercion of one form or another."[89] Edward P. Dozier writes, "Of all the missionary groups, the Mormons have made the most favorable impression; like the others, however, they have made few converts."[90]

Religious conversion aside, there is good evidence of reasonably peaceful cooperative Hopi-Mormon farming at Moenkopi for more than thirty-five years;[91] at Sunset, Arizona, near present Winslow, another cooperative farming experiment was destroyed in 1878 by floods rather than any cultural problems.[92] After criticizing the government's Moqui Agency in Keam's Canyon as being remote and useless, John G. Bourke wrote in 1884,

> I mention these facts to emphasize the difference between our slouchy ill-judged methods and the clean-cut, business-like ideas predominating in the Mormon management. The Latter-Day Saints are busy among the Moquis, and have met with considerable success. Their emissaries live *among* the Indians, and not forty miles away, and are constantly improving their opportunities for adding to an influence already considerable and not always friendly to the "Washington Great Father" [emphasis in original].[93]

On a personal level, the record shows that Haskell and Shelton got along well with the Orayvis. Both had lived with Indians before. Haskell called his Orayvi hosts "the best people I ever saw," while Shelton joined in their dances and referred to them amicably as "these folks," about whom he was trying to learn more. When Mormon missionaries next returned in December 1862, approaching Orayvi this time from the south, an unexpected direction, they were initially assumed to be a band of attacking Navajos, and hundreds of Orayvis prepared to give them a "warm reception"; however, "Brother Haskel[l] went ahead, and as soon as they saw him they commenced shaking hands with him, and fear gave place to joy among them."[94]

For the mission of 1862–63, Hamblin had to select three missionaries to stay the winter in Orayvi, and—as in 1859—he chose the three men—Ira Hatch, Jehiel McConnell, and Thales Haskell—according to his last-minute inspiration. When he heard his name called, Haskell "smiled over the news."[95]

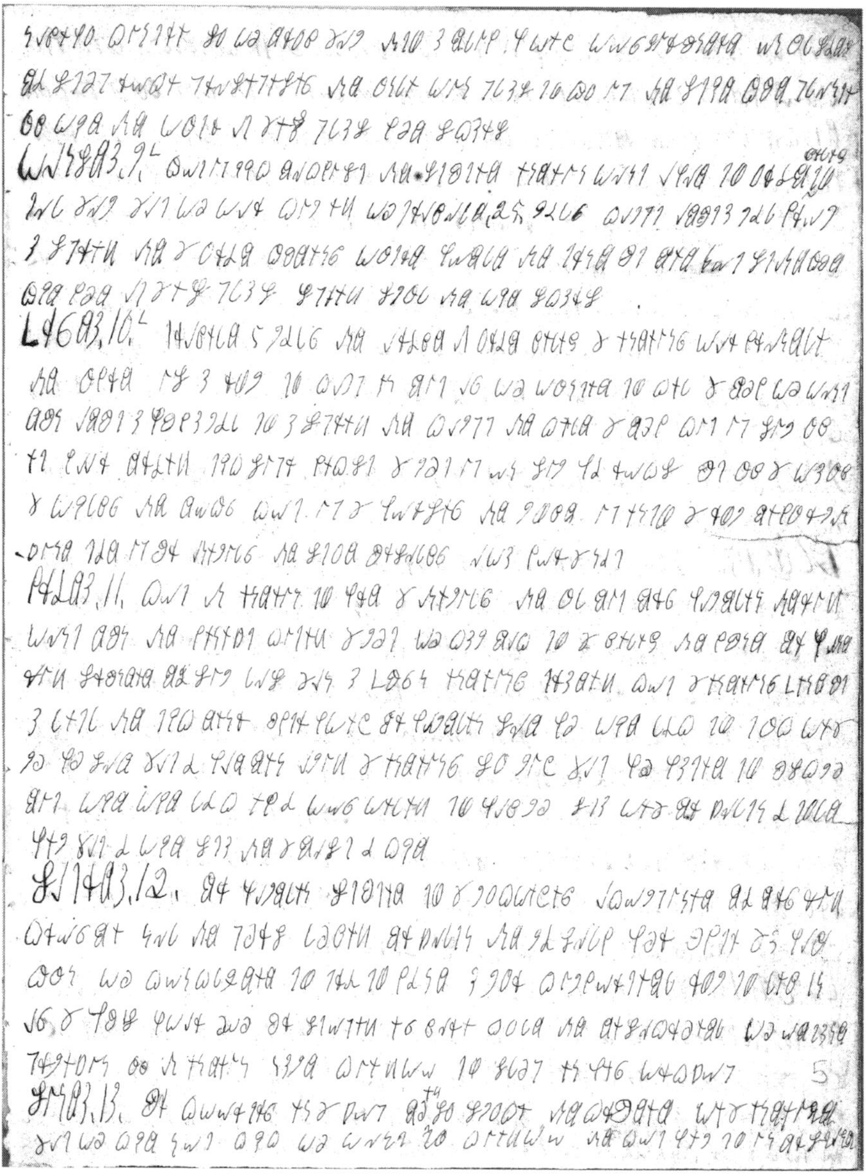

Figure 2.7. A page from Thales Haskell's journal, including the account of the missionaries' arrival in the Hopi village of Orayvi, written on Thursday, November 10, 1859. Courtesy L. Tom Perry Special Collections, Harold B. Lee Library, Brigham Young University, Provo, Utah.

2.3.3. Deseret Alphabet Handwriting and English Accents

The evidence that Marion Jackson Shelton collected the vocabulary during the 1859–60 Mormon mission to the Hopi is strong, but his companion Thales Haskell might also be a credible candidate. Haskell was with Shelton the whole time, was also studying the Hopi language, and even kept his own mission journal in the Deseret Alphabet to the end of 1859 (see Figure 2.7).

However, Kenneth Beesley, one of the authors of this book, has transcribed Haskell's 1859 Deseret Alphabet journal, and the handwriting of the vocabulary definitely does not match his. Deseret Alphabet texts, because they are written phonemically, also give strong clues to the accent of the writer, and here again Haskell looks less and less like the vocabulary author. For example, Haskell pronounced *dance* as /dɑns/, as in the south of England, while the writer of the vocabulary and Shelton pronounced it /dæns/, as in General American English. The word *ladder* shows up in the vocabulary, and in one of the Shelton letters to George A. Smith, written as ⱢⱵⱸⱤ (/lædr/), whereas Haskell always transcribed the same word in his journal with a low back vowel as ⱢⱸⱸⱤ (/lɑdr/), consistent with his origins in North New Salem, Massachusetts. Haskell also dropped his *r*s, at least after the low back /ɑ/ vowel, so his Deseret Alphabet spellings for words like *cart, bargain, started,* and *garment* lack the /r/-letter (Ɽ) completely (see Figure 2.8); there is no suggestion of such r-dropping in the vocabulary or in Shelton's Deseret Alphabet letters. Haskell also used a slightly unorthodox glyph ⱺ for the /ɔʲ/ diphthong in words like *boy,* while other writers at the time, including Shelton and the author of the vocabulary, used the standard 1859–60 glyph ⱺ.

While the historical evidence points strongly to Shelton, it must be noted that the Deseret-Alphabet handwriting of the known Shelton manuscripts and that of the vocabulary are not an obvious match.

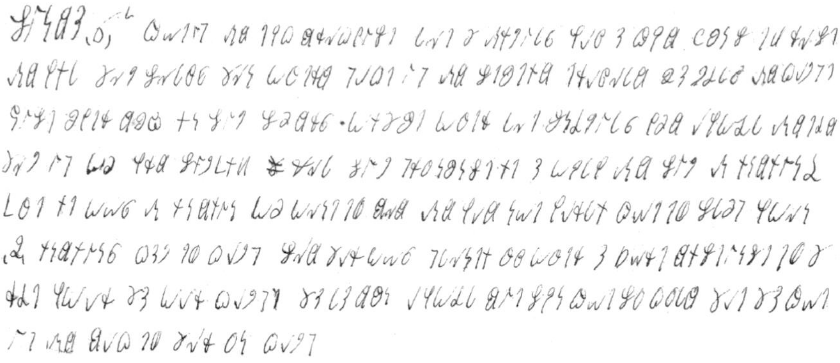

Figure 2.8. The entry from Thales Haskell's journal for Sunday, November 6, 1859. In the second line, the word *started*, written ꞩꞏꞓꞏꞆꜳ (/statɪd/), illustrates the way Haskell dropped his /r/s, at least after the /a/ vowel. Courtesy L. Tom Perry Special Collections, Harold B. Lee Library, Brigham Young University, Provo, Utah.

A comparison with the letter in Figure 2.6 shows systematic differences, especially in the shapes of the Ꝺ (/ʃ/) and ꞗ (/v/) letters. As shown in Figure 1.5, the vocabulary is very carefully written with almost no corrections, and the paper is in excellent condition. The surviving manuscript is probably a fair copy made either by Shelton himself, writing hypercarefully in a different hand, or more likely by a different clerk.

2.4. Mormon Interest in Native American Languages

Prominent Mormons showed a general and unusual interest in Native American languages at the time that the Deseret Alphabet was being promoted. The *Journal History* entry for November 15, 1853, records that W. W. Phelps, Dimick B. Huntington, Willard Richards (second counselor to Brigham Young), and others met to talk about "Indian Language, and the propriety of forming it in a book."

A number of the early Mormon missionaries had a marked gift for learning Indian languages, including Jacob Hamblin, Marion Shelton, Thales Haskell, Christian Lyngaa "Lingo" Christensen, and especially Ira Hatch, who allegedly spoke thirteen languages, married a Paiute woman (among other wives), and generally went native. In 1854, Dimick B. Huntington, who held the church office of Indian interpreter,[96] and was reported to have the "gift of tongues," was teaching "the Utah and Shoshone dialects" in Salt Lake City evening schools.[97] He also published a vocabulary of words in these languages, though not in the Deseret Alphabet.[98]

George W. Hill was called to the Salmon River Mission in April of 1855. According to his son, Joseph John Hill, he was "able to converse with the Indians in five different dialects" and was soon appointed interpreter for the mission.[99] In the 1870s, he acted as an interpreter for the government under Indian Agent Henry L. Dodge, and in 1877 he also published a vocabulary of the Shoshone language, using Roman letters rather than the Deseret Alphabet.[100] Yet another Shoshone vocabulary was published in Salt Lake City in 1859 by Joseph A. Gebow in Roman letters, but this was a non-Mormon effort, printed at the office of the *Valley Tan*, an anti-Mormon newspaper;[101] a second, "revised and improved," edition was published in 1864 by the *Daily Union Gazette* at Camp Douglas, the U.S. Army camp established near Salt Lake City.[102]

The LDS Church History Library has in its collection two versions of an anonymous Zuñi vocabulary written in Roman letters. Such vocabularies were probably copied and supplied to missionaries as aids to learning the languages. When the site for Fort Harmony, near modern New Harmony, Utah, was selected and dedicated, Brigham Young gave the following instructions to his Indian missionaries:

You are sent, not to farm, build nice houses and fence
fine fields, not to help white men, but to save the red
ones, learn their language, and you can do this more
effectively by living among them as well as by writing
down a list of words, go with them where they go, live
with them and when they rest let them live with you,
feed them, clothe them and teach them as you can, and
being thus with you all the time, you will soon be able
to teach them in their own language.[103]

2.5. Deseret Alphabet Orthographies for Native American Languages

Though the Deseret Alphabet was designed for English with letters
to represent the phonemes of English, Apostle Parley P. Pratt introduced it to his brother Orson with the optimistic claim that "this
alfabet [sic] will write Spanish, hebrew, greek; and, with the addition of a few more letters, all the Languages of the Earth."[104] Marion
J. Shelton also expressed the opinion that it could be used to write
Indian languages.[105]

On May 13, 1854, just a few months after the Deseret Alphabet
had been introduced to the public, Isaac Bullock was called on a
mission to the Shoshone in Wyoming. He collected a vocabulary
of Shoshone words and phrases in which some Shoshone pronunciations are indicated in the Deseret Alphabet. He also used the
Deseret Alphabet when trying to transcribe a few Spanish words.[106]
It is also clear that missionaries were routinely taught some survival Spanish, especially if they were heading for tribes in the south.
The journal of Andrew Smith Gibbons, who was a missionary to the
Hopi in 1858, contains a few useful Spanish phrases written in the
Deseret Alphabet, including the all-important *No me mates* ("Don't

kill me").[107] Marion Shelton was in fact engaged to teach Spanish in the southern Utah settlements, and his 1859 attempt to teach the Deseret Alphabet to the Paiutes, before the mission to the Hopi, has already been mentioned.[108] Over a period of at least twenty years, some Mormon missionaries had recourse to the Deseret Alphabet, and occasionally also Pitman shorthand, whenever they needed to transcribe Indian words "phonetically."

There are clues, requiring further research, that Mormon missionaries may have tried, however briefly, to take Deseret Alphabet-based literacy to the Navajo, Zuñi, Creek, Cherokee, and perhaps other tribes.[109] But it is clear that the initial enthusiasm soon faded. The period of 1859 to 1860 was one of unusual optimism and activity in the Deseret Alphabet movement, and there were very few missionaries like Marion Jackson Shelton who had studied shorthand and phonetics and were also proficient in the Deseret Alphabet. The English-Hopi vocabulary of 1859–60 may be a unique Deseret Alphabet survival. Even in Salt Lake City, the Deseret Alphabet reform was suspended in December 1860 and there is as yet no documented evidence of further attempts to teach it to Native Americans after this date.

2.6. Other Early Hopi Vocabularies

Shelton's 1860 vocabulary is the largest but not the only one from this early period. The earliest known Hopi vocabulary was collected by Army Lieutenant James H. Simpson. During a military reconnaissance through Navajo country, after concluding the Navaho Treaty of Canyon de Chelly, on September 9, 1849, he records,

> There was a Moqui Indian present at the council this morning as a spectator, and a more intelligent, frank-hearted looking fellow I have seldom beheld. Indeed, it

occurred to me that he had all the air and manner of a well-bred, vivacious American gentleman, and the only thing Indian in his appearance was his complexion. His people, whom he represents as living three days' travel from this place, have the *reputation* of being quite intelligent and orderly. [emphasis in original][110]

Simpson collected a list of thirty-nine "Moqui" words from this man, identified by expedition cartographer/illustrator Edward M. Kern as "CHE-KI-WAT-TE-WA, 'Yellow Wolf,'"[111] and they appear in Simpson's comparative vocabulary of Pueblo and other languages of the Southwest.[112]

After Shelton, Mosiah Lyman Hancock was a member of the Mormon 1862–63 mission to the Hopi, and he recorded that "I have been takeing down the Names of Many articles[.] I took it by what in those days was termed the Deseret Alphabet."[113] Unfortunately, his list has been lost.

John Wesley Powell collected about 370 Orayvi-dialect words in 1870,[114] and in 1873, John D. Lee collected sixty-seven Hopi words in Mùnqapi (Moenkopi), a satellite village of Orayvi.[115] Again in 1873, Henry Holmes, a member of the first Mormon company that attempted to settle the Little Colorado, visited the Hopi briefly and recorded in his journal a number of Hopi words in Pitman shorthand, including separate columns for "Oriba" (Orayvi, Third Mesa) and "Moqui" (First Mesa) words.[116] Andrew Amundsen, another member of the 1873 party, also visited the Hopi and wrote down some words using Roman letters, but they are largely illegible.[117]

Two decades later, in 1893, the Mennonite missionary and linguist H. R. Voth arrived in Orayvi and worked there for ten years. In addition to publishing a book on Hopi proper names and numerous ethnographic studies, he compiled an unpublished "English-Hopi Vocabulary" of thousands of words.[118] He was succeeded in Orayvi by J. B. Epp and other Mennonite missionaries, whose linguistic work, including an "English-Hopi & Hopi-English Dictionary," has been organized and collated by P. David Seaman.[119] We will return later to the early Mennonite manuscripts when trying to determine what Shelton's Deseret Alphabet spellings might have to say about the pronunciation of Hopi in Orayvi in 1860.

CHAPTER 3

Hopi Language

3.1. Hopi and the Uto-Aztecan Family

Hopi belongs to the Uto-Aztecan language family, which covers large portions of the western United States and neighboring Mexico. Besides Hopi, other well-known Uto-Aztecan languages include Nahuatl, Tarahumara, Yaqui, Ute, Paiute, Shoshone, and Comanche.

Taxonomically, Hopi occupies an interesting, semi-isolated place in the Uto-Aztecan language family tree since it is not closely related to the other Uto-Aztecan languages (see Figure 3.1). However, it is important not to make too much of this fact because Hopi speakers have been in more or less constant contact with other Uto-Aztecan speakers to the north and west—mostly Paiutes and Utes—as well as with non-Uto-Aztecan puebloans to the east. The Hopi are the only Uto-Aztecan speakers who adopted the puebloan lifestyle.

Words in Hopi are frequently made up of more than one meaningful part, or *morpheme*, giving rise to complex words. Morphologically complex words can be formed through affixation, reduplication, and compounding. Sound changes, such as vowel lengthening and shortening, elision, consonant alternations, and accentual shifts, often accompany these word-formation processes.

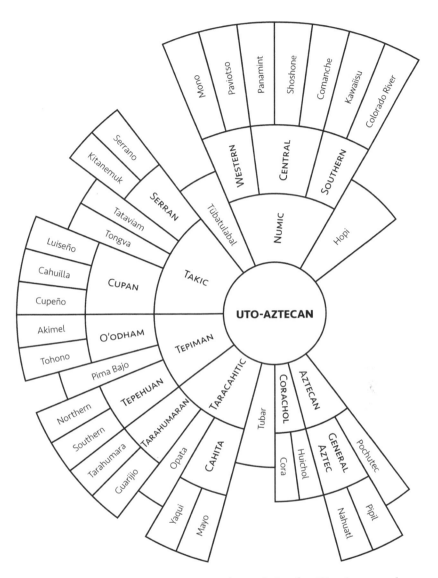

Figure 3.1. Hopi occupies its own branch in the Uto-Aztecan language family. The Numic/Southern/Colorado-River language is a dialect chain that stretches from southeastern California to Colorado, including Cheme-huevi, Southern Paiute, and Ute. Chart by Kurt Madsen.

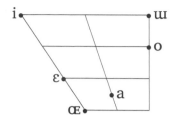

Figure 3.2. The Hopi short vowels.

Hopi sentences typically end with the verb, which is preceded by the subject and (when present) the object, in that order. The verbal word is capable of subtle nuances of tense, aspect, and modality, which in English typically require auxiliary or "helping" verbs.

3.2. Phonology

3.2.1. Hopi Vowels

The Hopi short vowels are shown in Figure 3.2, generally following the description in the *Hopi Dictionary—Hopìikwa Lavàytutveni*.[1] The vowel system is asymmetrical, which is common for northern Uto-Aztecan languages. Vowel length is partially an unpredictable property of the word in which it is found and partially predictable on phonotactic grounds. In the *Hopi Dictionary—Hopìikwa Lavàytutuveni* orthography, /i/ is written as <i>, /ɛ/ as <e>, /œ/ as <ö>, /a/ as <a>, /o/ as <o>, and /ɯ/ as <u>. Long vowels are orthographically doubled; e.g., /piːki/ ('bread') is spelled <piiki>. There are also a number of diphthongs that are not a factor here.

The vowel written <u> in the orthography has been variously described as a high central unrounded vowel [ɨ][2] or as a high back spread vowel [ɯ]. English speakers can approximate it by pronouncing the /ʊ/ vowel in *book* but with lips spread. The vowel written <ö> has been described as [œ],[3] as in the French word *veuve* or the more open [œ]. We use the descriptions of these vowels as found in the *Hopi Dictionary—Hopìikwa Lavàytutuveni*,[4] but nothing crucial hinges on this decision.

Using the Deseret Alphabet, Shelton had predictable trouble transcribing the high back spread /ɯ/ and the low front rounded /œ/ Hopi phonemes, which are quite different from anything heard in English or Spanish. He also had inconsistent sensitivity to Hopi vowel length, although his use of Deseret Alphabet "Long Vowels" vs. "Short Vowels" (see Figure 2.2) often corresponds to the Hopi length distinctions.

3.2.2. Hopi Consonants

There are twenty-one distinctive consonants in Hopi, as shown in Table 3.1. The Hopi consonant represented in the modern ortho-graphy as <ts> and usually described as [tˢ] is consistently tran-scribed in the vocabulary as Ɔ (/tʃ/), although the digraph ʇS (/ts/) could have been used. Perhaps Shelton perceived that it was a single phoneme in Hopi phonology and decided to transcribe it with the closest single Deseret Alphabet letter. But the vocabulary transcrip-tion may be quite reasonable phonetically; as noted by LaVerne Masayesva Jeanne, a linguist and a Third-Mesa-dialect speaker, the

Table 3.1. Hopi Consonants

	Bilabial	Alveolar	Palatal	Palatalized Velar	Velar	Rounded Velar	Uvular	Rounded Uvular	Glottal
Stop	p	t		kʲ	k	kʷ	q	qʷ	ʔ
Affricate		tˢ							
Fricative	β	s, r							h
Nasal	m	n		ŋʲ	ŋ	ŋʷ			
Glide			j			w			
Lateral		l							

Hopi affricate is "/c/, whose phonetic realization is typically [ts] with some raising of the body of the tongue (suggesting [c])."[5]

Third-Mesa Hopi, as commonly described, has intervocalic [β], rather than [b] or [v],[6] and Shelton uses either Ɛl (<b>) or Ɓ (<v>) to spell it, as does standard Spanish orthography; it is known that Shelton spoke and even taught Spanish. Benjamin Lee Whorf noted that /v/, at least in Musangnuvi, was "unrounded and varies freely between bilabial and labiodental."[7] The vocabulary transcribes the word for *horse*, written <kawayo> in modern Hopi orthography, as ꝊΓƐꝆᲧꝨΓ (/kʌvaʲjʌ/), probably indicating that Shelton recognized the borrowing from Spanish <caballo> ([ka'βajo]) and heard the middle consonant as [β] rather than [w]. In entry 213, the diminutive form <kawayhoya> ('colt') is similarly transcribed as /kʌ.vaʲ.-ho.jʌ/. Either the words were still pronounced in a more Spanish-like way in 1860, or Shelton misheard them that way.

Hopi also has a /k/ vs. /q/ distinction that Shelton missed completely; both are transcribed as Ꝋ, i.e., /k/. Shelton also failed to transcribe glottal stops, which are full consonants in Hopi. In conclusion, Shelton's known background in Pitman shorthand, Deseret Alphabet, and Spanish and Native American languages, plus some obvious phonetic study, made him a better-than-average amateur field phonetician, but not an excellent one. Identifying the Hopi words, based on Shelton's Deseret Alphabet transcriptions, occasionally presents a challenge.

3.3. The Third-Mesa Hopi Dialect

3.3.1. Coda /p/

Internal phonological evidence shows that the vocabulary represents the Third-Mesa dialect, and until 1906 the only village on Third Mesa was Orayvi.[8] In particular, a number of the entries

Table 3.2. Third-Mesa Words with Coda /p/

English	Eng.-Hopi Vocabulary	Third Mesa	Second Mesa
here	/jep/	yep(eq)	yev
there	/pep/	pep	pev
always	/sʌ.tʃep.sɪ/	sutsep	sutsev
shirt	/nʌp.nɑ/	napna	navna
go look for	/hɛp.to/	hepto	hevto

consistently show a coda /p/ (i.e., syllable-final /p/) typical of the Third-Mesa dialect, where the other dialects have /v/, pronounced [ɸ] or [f] (see Table 3.2).

3.3.2. The /s/ Phoneme

The Hopi /s/ phoneme is usually transcribed in the vocabulary as Ɗ, which would be [ʃ] in IPA, but occasionally it is transcribed as Ŝ (/s/). Thus, the word for beans, <morivosi>, is written by Shelton as ꓘ0ꓵꓭ6O꓊Ɗ (/morivoʃɪ/), and the word for jackrabbit, <sowi>, is written as ƊO.ꓱ (/ʃo.i/).

There is general agreement that the Hopi /s/ differs from the English /s/, but the explanations vary. Jeanne writes that the Hopi /s/ is a voiceless "apico-alveolar fricative" and is, in the speech of some, "accompanied by a certain amount of raising in the body of the tongue," producing an effect similar to the "lamino-alveolar [š]."[9] (Jeanne's [š] is an alternate symbol for /ʃ/.) Similarly, H. R. Voth, in his Hopi-English vocabulary, wrote the 'bean' word as <morivoci>, noting in his alphabetic key that his <c> represented "a sound between s and sh."[10] In a personal communication, David Shaul stated that to pronounce the Hopi /s/, "the tongue is slightly more flat than an English /s/." Whatever the explanation, Jeanne cites the difference as the reason why Hopi words with /s/ have often been transcribed in English orthography with the <sh> digraph, as in the names of the villages on

Second Mesa: Songòopavi transcribed as "Shungopavi," Supawlavi as "Shipaulavi," and Musangnuvi as "Mishongnovi."

J. B. Epp, or one of the other Mennonite missionaries who succeeded Voth in Orayvi, claimed to have heard a gender difference in the pronunciation of <s>: "S is a sound very much like the English *for women*! Men give it a variety of sounds lying between s and sh. The tongue, too, takes position in the mouth between those of the s and sh positions."[11]

3.3.3. The /r/ Phoneme

3.3.3.1. Formal Linguistic Descriptions

The Hopi /r/ phoneme, and Shelton's Deseret Alphabet transcriptions of it, raise some interesting phonetic and perhaps even historical and ethnological questions. The phonetic questions are genuinely difficult, complicated by the variety of terminologies and phonetic symbols used by various linguists over the years and by a dearth of Hopi audio recordings and articulatory X-rays available for study. We will examine the evidence and make suggestions for future research.

Hopi is generally described as having four dialects:

1. First Mesa (1M), which is not well studied or described;

2. Second Mesa: Musangnuvi village (2MM);

3. Second Mesa: Songòopavi and Supawlavi villages, the "S-villages" (2MS);

4. Third Mesa, including Orayvi, Kiqötsmovi, Hotvela, Paaqavi, Upper Mùnqapi, and Lower Mùnqapi (3M).

Whorf, who worked on the Musangnuvi dialect in the 1940s, wrote that "r is untrilled, retroflex, and slightly spirantal."[12] The term spirantal is rarely used today, usually replaced by fricative, which describes those sounds "in which a turbulent airstream is produced within the vocal tract."[13]

Milo Kalectaca wrote a Hopi textbook based on his own Second-Mesa S-village dialect, and he describes the /r/ this way: "Hopi *r*, exemplified in *riya* 'spin', is not like the English *r*. It resembles the sound spelled by *s* in *measure*, by *z* in *azure*, and by *ge* in *rouge*, except that it is made in Hopi with the tip of the tongue turned up toward the roof of the mouth."[14] Similarly, Alfred F. Whiting, in a paper entitled "You can record Hopi," wrote the following:

> Hopi *r* will drive you out of your mind. It often sounds like *rz*, or just plain *z*. This sound is made without any real trill (contrast Spanish *r*), but with the tip of the tongue turned back towards the roof of the mouth. If you hear something that sounds like a*z*ure, a *z* or *rz* or *zr*, it is probably nothing more than a plain Hopi *r* and can be recorded as "r".[15]

The <s> in *measure*, the <z> in *azure*, and the <ge> in *rouge*, referred to by Kalectaca and Whiting, represent a somewhat rare English phoneme, denoted /ʒ/ in IPA, that occurs also in *treasure*, *pleasure, leisure, vision, precision,* and *closure.* Peter Ladefoged and Ian Maddieson note that the place of articulation for /ʒ/ and its voiceless counterpart /ʃ/ has been described by several well-known phoneticians as either "palato-alveolar" or "alveolo-palatal," refer-ring to a region between the alveolar ridge and the hard palate.[16] There is general agreement, whatever the terminology, that the place of articulation is posterior to the alveolar ridge, where the English /t/, /d/, /n/, /s/ and /z/ are articulated; Ladefoged and Maddieson settled on the term *postalveolar*, which is also used by the International Phonetic Association,[17] noting that in other languages, the postalveolar area needs to be divided into palato-alveolar and

alveolo-palatal regions. While the English /ʒ/ is generally considered to be laminal—articulated with the blade rather than the tip
of the tongue—X-ray studies reveal considerable variation among
English speakers in the position of the tongue when pronouncing
/ʒ/ and /ʃ/: either with the tip up, resulting in a more apical con-
striction, or with the tip down, resulting in a more laminal constric-
tion; in either case, the general front of the tongue must be raised,
and Ladefoged and Maddieson use the term *domed*.[18]

The English /ʒ/ is a voiced fricative, involving a primary con-
striction between the tongue and the postalveolar region that produces a jet of air that then strikes a secondary obstacle, the teeth,
producing a high-frequency hissy turbulence. Such hissy articula-
tions are known as sibilants (or, equivalently, stridents). Ladefoged
and Maddieson therefore categorize the /ʒ/ as a voiced postalveolar
domed sibilant fricative.[19] The *Handbook of the International Phonetic
Association* describes /ʒ/ as a "voiced postalveolar fricative," with
"fricative" here, as in many other descriptions, implying the sibilance as well.[20]

The voiceless counterpart of the English /ʒ/ is the /ʃ/, usually
represented in English orthography by <sh>, as in *ship* and *fish*;
this /ʃ/ is often pronounced with a degree of lip rounding, which
lowers the pitch and helps to distinguish /ʃ/ from /s/ acoustically.

It is important to note that Kalectaca, among others, states only
that the Hopi /r/ in words like *riya* "resembles" the English /ʒ/; that
is, it is acoustically the closest phoneme that one can find in English.
The key difference, he claims, is that the Hopi /r/ is produced with
"the tip of the tongue turned up toward the roof of the mouth";
such an articulation is called retroflex (or equivalent terms) in more
formal descriptions.

Since the time of Whorf, Whiting, and Kalectaca, most linguists have described the Hopi /r/ as having two distinct allophones (contextual variants of a phoneme):

1. A voiced allophone, often compared to the English /ʒ/, that occurs in the context before a vowel, as in Kalectaca's *riya* example, or as in *kyaaro* ('parrot');

2. A voiceless allophone, often compared to the English /ʃ/, that occurs in other contexts, as in *Kyarngyam* ('parrot clan').

Given the facts of Hopi phonology, the voiced /r/s that occur before vowels are also syllable initial, while the other, voiceless /r/s are in syllable-final or coda position.

Thus Ekkehart Malotki compares the /r/ in "syllable initial position" to the *s* in *leisure*, i.e., the /ʒ/ cited by Kalectaca, and further specifies the articulation as "with tongue tip curled toward palate"; but the /r/ in "syllable final position" he compares to the *sh* in English *ship*, i.e., /ʃ/ in the IPA.[21]

Even in *Coyote & the Winnowing Birds*, a children's book edited by the late Emory Sekaquaptewa, a Hopi speaker from Hotvela on Third Mesa, and Barbara Pepper, the authors devote two pages to the subject of /r/, writing that

> Hopi has two consonant sounds that are written like the English *r*, but pronounced very differently.
>
> *r* followed by a vowel has a "zh" sound, something like the *s* in "measure," or the *z* in "azure." This *r* is called the voiced *r*....
>
> *r* not followed by a vowel sounds like "sh" but with the tongue curled up toward the roof of the mouth. This *r* is called an unvoiced *r*.[22]

In "A Sketch of Hopi Grammar," by Kenneth C. Hill and Mary E. Black, an appendix to the *Hopi Dictionary—Hopìikwa Lavàytutuveni*, the two allophones of /r/ are described as

- [z̢] "before a vowel: voiced apico-alveolar fricative (something like a cross between Spanish *rr* and the sound in the middle of English *vision*)";

- [ʂ] "at the end of a syllable: a voiceless apico-alveolar fricative (somewhat as *rsh* in *harsh*) [In the Second Mesa speech of Shipaulovi and Shungopavi (cf. Kalectaca 1978) syllable-final *r* is replaced by *s*.]"[23]

The term *apico-alveolar* refers to sounds articulated with the tip of the tongue touching or near the alveolar ridge; most other linguists have described the Hopi /r/ allophones, at least on Third Mesa, as being retroflex (or apico-domal), which involves a place of articulation behind the alveolar ridge. However, Hill and Black use the IPA characters [z̢] and [ʂ] with the "retroflex hook," which is standard notation for the voiced and voiceless retroflex sibilants.

Using the [z̢] and [ʂ] symbols, <mori> ('beans'), with /r/ before a vowel, is commonly pronounced ['moz̢i], and, similarly, <Orayvi> is pronounced [ʔoˈz̢aʲβi] and <kyaaro> ('parrot') is ['kʲaːz̢o]; in contrast, the words <Kyarngyam> ('Parrot Clan') and <kyarwungwa> ('Parrot Clan member'), where the /r/s are syllable final, are pronounced ['kʲaʂŋʲam] and ['kʲaʂwuŋwa], respectively, i.e., with the voiceless [ʂ].

For most Hopi speakers, both of these fricative allophones of /r/ are also sibilant (also called strident), involving a primary restriction that directs a jet of air toward the sharp edge of the teeth, which are held close together, providing a secondary obstacle "downstream" that creates further hissy turbulence. The English /ʒ/ and /ʃ/, often cited as the English phonemes most resembling the two Hopi allophones of /r/, are also sibilant fricatives. But as noted by Ladefoged and Maddieson, "at some points within the vocal tract it is possible to form two different constrictions, one that will produce a sibilant fricative, and one that will produce a non-sibilant fricative." The difference, they explain, can involve an apical/laminal distinction, different shapes of the tongue, different sizes of the channel producing the jet of air, and how closely the teeth are held together. For example, if "the teeth are fairly far apart," they "do not form an obstruction" that produces sibilance.[24]

In 1964, Guy Tyler visited the Hopi reservation and made some audio recordings of Mrs. Monongye (Monongya) in Orayvi.[25] Mrs. Monongya pronounced *Orayvi* with what appears to be a postalveolar fricative or approximant that is not sibilant. Dirk Elzinga analyzed a spectrogram of this recording, which shows the turbulence associated with fricatives quite clearly. It also revealed her /r/ allophone in *Orayvi* to be retroflex, at least partially voiced, and, for Anglophones, rhotic in quality.[26]

LaVerne Masayesva Jeanne also describes the two allophones of /r/ in her dissertation but claims that the allophone of /r/ before a vowel can be pronounced "in a variety of ways," including a "light tap" that is not mentioned by other linguists: "The sole remaining 'liquid', the rhotic written /r/, is produced in a variety of ways, ranging from an extremely light tap [r][27] to a retroflexed, i.e. apico-domal, fricative [ẓ], with the latter allophone predominating.[28] This consonant is voiced except in syllable-final position where it is regularly a voiceless apico-domal fricative [ṣ]."[29]

The only other possible reference to tapped /r/s, described using the ambiguous term *trilling*, that we have found is in the vocabulary by "J. B. Epp and other Mennonite Missionaries," collated by P. David Seaman:

Trying to sound rzh together as one sound as nearly as possible brings one near to it. When r is initial then the

ehrilling [*sic* in typescript, for trilling], as in German and
Spanish, is heard quite distinctly; but when final then
only a touch of a thrill [*sic*, for trill] can be perceived,
almost all of the sound is then xh or sh. For this reason
many Hopi words are being written with sh or s that
should have r in those places.[30]

Since Epp mistranscribed the coda /r/ as <s>,[31] this description
was probably written by J. B. Frey, J. R. Duerksen, or some other
successor in the Mennonite mission.

Some years before finding these descriptions by Jeanne and
the Mennonite missionaries, author Beesley was surprised to hear
the prevocalic /r/ pronounced as a clear Spanish-like tap by one
speaker from Supawlavi and several speakers from Orayvi, one of
whom actually corrected him when he said [ʔoˈzaʲβi], insisting on
[ʔoˈraʲβi]. The prevocalic "tappers" nevertheless pronounced the
/r/ in syllable-final position as the voiceless retroflex sibilant fricative [ʂ], so the word <kyaaro> ('parrot') was pronounced [ˈkʲaːɾo]
while the related word <Kyarngyam> ('Parrot Clan') was pronounced [ˈkʲaʂŋʲam]. Some modern speakers in Orayvi may have
as many as four allophones for /r/, but this requires further study.

1. [ɹ] or [ɻ] at the beginning of a word: riyànpi [ɹiˈjànpi];

2. [ɾ] or [ɽ] in the context vowel-r-vowel: Orayvi [ʔoˈraʲβi];

3. [ʂ] at the end of a syllable: Kyarngyam [ˈkʲaʂŋʲam]; and

4. [ʐ] in the context consonant-r-vowel: momri [ˈmomʐi].

3.3.3.2. Shelton's Transcription of Hopi /r/ using the Deseret Alphabet

In the 1860 English-Hopi Vocabulary, the /r/ in Hopi words is consistently transcribed by Shelton as

1. 𐐡, the Deseret Alphabet /r/ letter, before a vowel, or

2. 𐐠, the Deseret Alphabet /s/ letter, at the end of a syllable.

Although, as we have seen, the Hopi /r/ before vowels has often been compared to the English voiced postalveolar sibilant /ʒ/ heard in words like *measure* and *azure*, Shelton never uses the Deseret Alphabet 𐐠 letter (representing the English /ʒ/) when transcribing Hopi words. In the many words in the vocabulary containing /r/ before a vowel, such as <morivosi> ('beans'), he always transcribes them with the Deseret Alphabet 𐐡 letter originally intended to represent the English /r/.

The vocabulary includes only three words with syllable-final /r/, and all of them are transcribed with the Deseret Alphabet 𐐠 (/s/) letter: <wùutiharku> ('old woman') is transcribed as 𐐎𐐳𐐻𐐮.𐐸𐐰𐑅.𐐿𐐲 (/wʊh.tɪ.hʌs.kʌ/); <piyarhoya> ('fawn kid') is transcribed as 𐐑𐐯.𐐰𐑅.-𐐸𐐬.𐐷𐐲 (/pi.æs.ho.jʌ/); and <momorya>, ('be swimming') is transcribed as 𐐊𐐬.𐐊𐐬.𐑅𐐮.𐐷𐐰 (/mo.mo.sɪ.jæ/). Recall that the Hopi /s/ phoneme, discussed earlier, was generally, but not always, transcribed by Shelton as 𐐊 (/ʃ/).

Given Shelton's limited exposure to Hopi and the lack of example pairs like *kyaaro/Kyarngyam*, it is highly unlikely that he recognized that he was using the 𐐡 (/r/) and 𐐠 (/s/) letters to represent the same phoneme. Judging by Shelton's consistent choice of the available Deseret Alphabet letters, it is reasonable to assume that he heard the prevocalic /r/ in 1860 Orayvi as rhotic and probably nonsibilant, while he heard the /r/ in syllable-final position as something definitely sibilant, probably [ʂ]. The prevocalic /r/s of his informants may have been nonsibilant voiced fricatives, as in the speech of Mrs. Monongya, or taps.

We have no idea how many informants Shelton worked with, and his journal, which might have shed light on this question, is lost. We only know, from Haskell's journal, that Shelton spent almost all of his time in Orayvi, with only brief excursions to Songòopavi and Supawlavi on Second Mesa and to the "Moquitch Village," which was probably Wàlpi/Sitsom'ovi, on First Mesa. We know also that Shelton and Haskell interacted regularly with Kuyngwu, and somewhat with Tuuvi, in Orayvi and lived with unmarried men in the Wikwlapi kiva, with which Kuyngwu and Tuuvi were associated.[32] Complicating the dialect picture is the matriarchal nature of Hopi society and the practice of exogamy, which requires people to marry outside their clan (and clan set), so that a married man moves into the household of his wife, perhaps in a different village where a different dialect is spoken.

3.3.3.3. The Mennonite Orthography for /r/

In 1893, the Mennonite missionary H. R. Voth arrived in Orayvi and started studying the language. He collected a large vocabulary of Hopi words and soon after published a book of Hopi proper names, where the word for parrot—spelled <kyaaro> in the *Hopi Dictionary—Hopìikwa Lavàytutuveni*—is written as <ǩáro>.[33] But proper names on the same page, identified clearly as based on the 'parrot' word and with the /r/ in syllable-final position, show those /r/s written as < rzh >, e.g., <Ǩárzhwaima> ('Parrot Walks'), where he identifies the root as "ditto" (meaning <ǩáro>) and the suffix as < wáima >: 'walk, go straight forward.' This suggests that Voth knew that his <r> before vowels, and his <rzh> in coda position, represented the same phoneme. It is hardly conceivable that Voth could have known about Shelton's Deseret Alphabet vocabulary or been influenced by it, but like Shelton, he transcribed the /r/ before vowels simply as < r >, while the /r/s in syllable-final position he wrote as < rzh >, likely to reflect a sibilant [ʂ].

Voth left after ten years in Orayvi and in 1916 his successor, J. B. Epp, published *Bible History in the Hopi Indian Language* in an orthography that uses <r> for the prevocalic /r/ and, it seems, just <s> for the coda /r/. These conventions are completely parallel to Marion Shelton's, and it seems unlikely that Epp realized, in 1916, that he was dealing with a single /r/ phoneme. The Mennonite vocabulary includes the 'old woman' word, written <wùutiharku> in the *Hopi Dictionary—Hopìikwa Lavàytutuveni*, which is rendered as <wúhti-hasku>, very parallel to Shelton's Deseret Alphabet spelling 𐐎𐐋𐑁.𐐆𐐻.𐑁𐑉𐐝.𐐉𐑉 (/wʊh.tɪ.hʌs.kʌ/).[34]

By 1924, however, a subsequent Mennonite Bible-study book appeared,[35] again using <r> for prevocalic /r/ but now consistently using the digraph <rs> for syllable-final /r/, a convention that has been used ever since in the Mennonite orthography, including the 1972 Wycliffe translation of the Hopi New Testament.[36] So it appears that the Mennonite missionaries, at least by 1924, realized that there was just one /r/ phoneme, but they retained the *s* in their orthographical convention <rs> to reflect the sibilance in the syllable-final allophone. Jonathan Ekstrom, who supervised the translation of the New Testament into Hopi and wrote, with his first wife, the book *How to Read and Write Hopi* about the Mennonite orthography, is completely aware that the <r> and <rs> represent the same phoneme.

The orthographical conventions used by Mormon and Mennonite missionaries to Orayvi raise a number of questions that deserve further research. Ideally a survey should be conducted to determine the range of pronunciations of /r/ on the Third Mesa today and see if they vary according to age, sex, or village.

3.3.4. Third-Mesa Dialect Words

In addition to the systematic phonological differences already discussed, the vocabulary lists a number of word forms that indicate the Third-Mesa dialect (see Table 3.3).

Table 3.3. Third-Mesa Dialect Words

1860 English-Hopi Vocabulary	Other Dialects
koho	kwuhu (Second Mesa)
putskoho	putskwuhu
kolaasa	koraasa (Musangnuvi)

3.3.5. Modern Third-Mesa Falling Tone

Perhaps the most interesting examples from the 1860 vocabulary are the transcriptions of words that in modern Third-Mesa dialect are generally described as having a falling tone (see Table 3.4). Shelton had no way to indicate tone using the Deseret Alphabet and perhaps would not have heard it; a number of syllables with modern falling tone—mostly <ùu> but one example of <ìi> and one of <àa>— are clearly transcribed in the vocabulary with a vowel followed by a coda /h/-letter.[37]

The *Hopi Dictionary—Hopìikwa Lavàytutuveni*, which records the modern Third-Mesa dialect, indicates that words such as <wùuti> ('woman') are pronounced with a falling tone on the Third Mesa;[38] with a long vowel but with no distinguishing tone in the Second-Mesa dialect of Supawlavi and Songòopavi, i.e., <wuuti>; and as <wuhti>, with coda /h/, or a preaspirated /t/, in the Second-Mesa village of Musangnuvi[39] and perhaps on First Mesa, where the dialect is less studied.[40]

The examples in Table 3.4 suggest that the 1859–60 Third-Mesa pronunciation was more like that of the modern Musangnuvi dialect and proto-Uto-Aztecan;[41] if so, the development of the Third-Mesa phenomenon of falling tone is relatively recent. Alexis Manaster-Ramer came to that conclusion after studying the oldest Hopi data then available, dating from circa 1900 and the 1930s.[42] However, some other words with modern Third-Mesa falling tone are not transcribed by Shelton with a coda /h/, as shown in Table 3.5.

Table 3.4. Words with Modern Third-Mesa Falling Tone

English	1860 Vocab.	Kroeber	Third-Mesa Orthog.
woman	wʊh.tɪ	wöxti	wùuti
old-man	wʊh.tʌk.ʌ	wöx-daka	wùutaqa
old-woman	wʊh.tɪ.hʌs.kʌ		wùutiharku
tracks	kʊh.kʊ.ɪ.tʌ		kùuku'yta
broil	tʊh.pɛ		tùupe
your	ʊh		u-, ùu-, uu-
shut	ʊh.taʲ		ùuta
surround	ʊh-taʲ.jʌ		ùuta(~ya)
suit, befit	ʃʊ.ɪn.ɪh.pɛ		sú-'inùu-pe
like	ʃʊ.hɪ.joŋ.wɒ		sùuyongwa(~ya)
be many, extra	nih.tɪ.jo.tʌ		nìitiw|ta
rejoice	hɑh.laʲt.ʌ		hàalayti

Note: These words are transcribed in Deseret Alphabet with a coda (syllable-final) /h/-letter. The examples from Kroeber's survey of California Shoshonean languages suggest that the pronunciations with some kind of velar frication, [h] or [x], are older and that the development of the modern Hopi Third-Mesa-dialect falling tone is relatively recent.

While the examples are inconsistent, it is hard to imagine that Shelton used the coda-/h/ spelling as some kind of orthographical convention to represent falling tone. He was simply trying to write down what he heard as best he could, using the letters provided by the Deseret Alphabet. So where he did use the coda /h/, we need to entertain the possibility that he really heard something like /h/.

There are two other entries in the vocabulary that also suggest an earlier, pre–falling-tone pronunciation. The *Hopi Dictionary— Hopìikwa Lavàytutuveni* lists the modern Third-Mesa words for 'little boy' and 'little girl' as <tiyòoya> and <manàwya>, respectively: each, according to the *Dictionary*, involves the diminutive suffix usually appearing as <-hoya>, with <tiyòoya> being <tiyo> 'boy' + <-`ya>, a variant of <-hoya> used after /o/; and <manàwya> being

Table 3.5. Other Words with Third-Mesa Falling Tone

English	1860 Vocab.	Modern 3rd-Mesa Orthography
back-bone	hot.æt	hòota('at) (back, body part)
old	wʌ.jo.tʌ	wuyòoti
year	jæ.ʃæŋ.vʊ	yàasangw
trade	hʊ-ɪ-jʌ	hùuya (i.)
comb	wʊ.ʃɪ	wùusi
card (verb)	ʃe.kʌn.tʌ	sòöqanta (i.)
fox	ʃɪ.kjæ.taʲ	sikyàatayo (red fox)
forget	ʃʊ.to.kɪ	sùutoki
sneeze	ɑ.ʃi.	àasi(k-)
straighten	tʃe.kwʌn.tʌ	tsìikwanta
little	hi-ʃaʲ.jʌ	hìisay

Note: These words with modern Third-Mesa falling tone were not transcribed by Shelton in the 1860 vocabulary with a coda /h/-letter. The lack of coda /h/ in these examples may simply reflect inconsistent transcription or a sound change in progress.

<maana> 'girl' + <-ˋwya>, a variant used after other vowels.[43] Jeanne proposes that the modern Third-Mesa word is phonetically [manáhʷya].[44] On Second Mesa, <manahoya> and <tiyohoya> are still heard.

The English-Hopi vocabulary (see entries 359 and 360) shows these two words transcribed as /ti.o.hwi.jʌ/ and /mɑ.nɑ.hwi.jʌ/ (Deseret Alphabet 𐐞𐐬.𐐄.𐐿𐐶𐐘.𐑅𐑉 and 𐐫𐐞.𐐨𐐬.𐐿𐐶𐐘.𐑅𐑉), which appears to involve an earlier common diminutive suffix */-hwija/, or perhaps just a misheard standard diminutive suffix /-hoja/, used after both /o/ and /a/. But here, taken at face value, is something very similar to the suffix "*-hʷya" postulated as an intermediate form by Jeanne.[45] Relatively recent productive alternations of /V+h/ sequences to long falling-tone vowels /V̀V/ could account for the modern Third-Mesa pronunciations.[46]

In Voth's "Hopi-English Vocabulary," also compiled in Orayvi, he, too, used a coda-/h/ spelling where the modern Third-Mesa dialect has falling tone, and this spelling persists as a convention in the Mennonite orthography today. In his "Vocabulary," in a table entitled "Alphabet & rules for pronounciation [*sic*]," Voth wrote that the *h* was pronounced "at end of silable [*sic*] like a soft German 'ch'."[47]

In the Mennonite vocabulary, the 'woman' word (<wùuti> in the *Hopi Dictionary—Hopìikwa Lavàytutuveni*) is written <wúhti>, and in a section entitled "Notes on the Grammar of the Hopi Language by the Mennonite Missionaries," the pronunciation of <h> is described thus: "H when at the beginning of a syllable it is unmarked and has the sound of h as in English. At the end of a syllable it has all the shades of the h sound, from a mere breath to the sound of the Greek x or the German ch as in ach!. When it has this latter sound it is marked thus ḣ."[48]

Author Elzinga has analyzed some available audio recordings of modern Third-Mesa speakers, including Mrs. Monongya, who pronounce words such as <wùuti>, <wùutiharku>, <manàwya>, and <tiyòoya> with a clear pitch drop (i.e., falling tone) but no discernible velar friction, devoicing, or breathy voice. It is likely that the historical progression of Third-Mesa pronunciation for words such as <wuhti>/<wùuti> went from the aspiration or fricatives apparently heard by Voth, Epp, and Shelton (pronunciations that are still heard today in the Musangnuvi dialect), to some kind of breathy voice or devoicing, to the modern falling-tone pitch drop. Some Third-Mesa speakers may well have remnants of breathy voice or devoicing, and ideally a survey could be conducted.

CHAPTER 4

The 1860 English-Hopi Vocabulary

4.1. English-Hopi Entries

The entire 1860 English-Hopi vocabulary is reproduced in this book, comprising 486 original English-Hopi entries, plus transcriptions into the International Phonetic Alphabet and references to the words in modern Hopi dictionaries.

Of the 486 entries, a relatively small number remain mysterious or at least questionable and deserve further study.[1] The challenges include scribal errors in the Deseret Alphabet (e.g., see entry 467), general copying errors, switching two terms (e.g., see entries 476 and 477, where the glosses for *flint* and *steel* are reversed), perhaps ephemeral slang and obsolete terms, and examples of what philosopher W. V. O. Quine called the "indeterminacy of translation."[2] Quine considered the challenges of a field linguist, such as Marion J. Shelton, trying to record a previously unknown language. If a rabbit runs by, and a native speaker points to it and says "gavagai," the possible meanings or translations include

Rabbit.
Lo, a rabbit.
Lo, a mammal.

Lo, an animal.

Lo, food.

Let's go hunting.

Gray.

It runs.

Illustrating such a gavagai confusion, the vocabulary includes *curls* (entry 229), glossed clearly as *kanelhoya*, which means 'lamb.' One can imagine Shelton pointing at a lamb's wool, hoping to elicit the Hopi word for curls but getting the word for lamb instead. Other gavagai problems might appear in the entries for *blunt* (156), *dancing* (182), *mad* (398), *buffalo robe* (469), and perhaps *sister* (286).

4.2. Notable Entries

A few of the vocabulary entries are especially notable. The Hopi word that Shelton heard for paper (entry 90) translates as "writing cornhusks," while one of the words for the cards used to card wool (entry 217) translates as "cat's tongue" (<moslengi>). Cards are wooden paddles covered on one side with hundreds or thousands of little wire hooks that tease out and straighten the wool fibers. Anyone who has ever been licked by the raspy tongue of a cat will appreciate the metaphor. The longest and most elaborate translation is for "hickory shirt" (entry 110), a kind of heavy cotton work shirt with narrow vertical blue and white stripes that can still be bought today. Farmers have long used hickory shirts and hickory overalls, and these shirts were among the trade goods offered by the missionaries. Cotton cloth in the "hickory weave" has also been used in work clothing for machinists, lumberjacks, and especially railroad engineers. Shelton's informant rendered hickory shirt as roughly "blue striped-with-several-stripes manufactured-cloth shirt."

APPENDIX A

Hopi Locations

A.1. The Moquitch Village

While nineteenth-century Mormons and other outsiders often used the terms Moqui, Moki, Moquee, Moquis, Moquich, or Moquitch to refer collectively to all the Hopi people, numerous early Mormon usages of these terms clearly refer more specifically to the villages and people of First Mesa. The Oraibis or Oribes, residents of the Third-Mesa village of Orayvi, are often distinguished from the Moquis or Moquitches, the residents of the Moquis/Moquitch village.

Andrew Smith Gibbons indicates that the four missionaries of 1858 were originally left by Jacob Hamblin in what Gibbons called "the Moquis village" under the jurisdiction of "the Moquis chief," and he estimated the "oriba village" to be eighteen miles away;[1] this distance is consistent only with a First-Mesa village. During the 1859–60 mission, Thales Haskell, living in Orayvi, underestimated "the Moquis village," which he had not visited, to be ten miles away.[2] There were, and still are, three villages on top of First Mesa: Wàlpi, Sitsom'ovi, and Hanoki, which is also called the Tewa Village. This raises the question: Which First-Mesa village was the Moquis/Moquitch village or which First-Mesa villages were grouped together as the Moquis/Moquitch village? The evidence is mixed.

When Major John Wesley Powell visited the Hopi villages in 1870, guided by Jacob Hamblin, he explicitly referred collectively to all three of the First-Mesa villages—Wàlpi, Sitsom'ovi, and even Hanoki—as "the Moqui Towns."[3]

In 1873, John Hanson Beadle described the Moqui village in a way that can only indicate Sitsom'ovi on First Mesa.[4] However, Beadle is not completely reliable—he idiosyncratically uses the name Moquina for the village next to Sitsom'ovi, and he places a village he calls Hualpec—obviously a form of the name Wàlpi, which is the village next to Sitsom'ovi on First Mesa—on Second Mesa. (The villages on Second Mesa are Songòopavi, Supawlavi, and Musangnuvi.) In 1872, Clement Powell also seemed to equate the Moquis village with Sitsom'ovi.[5]

Shortly after the 1859–60 mission, Thomas Bullock prepared two maps of the route from Fort Clara, now Santa Clara, Utah, and nearby Washington City to the Hopi Villages.[6] The second of the maps, "the places, distances, and courses, being given by Jacob Hamblin, same day, from recollection," clearly labels as Moquitch what looks to be the Wàlpi village on First Mesa.

It is very possible that the early missionaries were referring to two villages—Wàlpi and Sitsom'ovi—collectively as the Moqui, Moquis, or Moquitch village. This was clearly the case with U.S. Army Captain A. H. Palmer, special agent to the Moquis pueblo Indians, who in 1869 carefully listed all of the Hopi villages and the population of each, but he identified only two villages on First Mesa: Moqui and Te-ua.[7] His Te-ua is clearly the Tewa village, also known as Hanoki, where the so-called Hopi-Tewa people, who speak the Tewa language, live; his Moqui village, therefore, conflates Wàlpi and Sitsom'ovi.

The political situation on First Mesa is, and probably was, just as confusing. Wàlpi, the oldest settlement, is considered the "mother village" of First Mesa, and Sitsom'ovi is described as its overflow or "suburb" village. Hanoki (Tewa) was settled by non-Hopi refugees from the Rio Grande after the Pueblo Revolt of 1680.[8] In 2014, the *kikmongwi* (village chief) of Wàlpi is generally regarded as the kikmongwi of all the First-Mesa villages, although Hanoki has its own leader for internal affairs. The duties, powers, and legitimacy of kikmongwis are much in question throughout all the Hopi villages.

Gibbons's "Moqui village" of 1858 was probably Wàlpi, including its overflow village of Sitsom'ovi; and his "Moquis chief" was probably the kikmongwi of Wàlpi.

A.2. Blue Canyon

During the third Mormon mission to the Hopi, on November 2, 1860, Hamblin and his missionary party were stopped in Blue Canyon on the Moenkopi Wash, one long day's travel from Orayvi, by a band of hostile Navajos and prevented from completing their journey. In the tense situation that followed, eighteen-year-old George A. Smith Jr., son of Mormon Apostle George A. Smith, was shot by arrows and bullets, apparently from his own revolver, and was paralyzed from the waist down.[9] The hostile Navajos scattered momentarily and Hamblin and his men hastily retreated north an estimated eight to eleven miles, pursued by perhaps a hundred hostile Navajos, and protected by four friendly Navajos, before young Smith died at sunset. The body had to be abandoned in "a hollow place by the side of the trail."[10]

In May 1938, the LDS Church erected a stone monument to George A. Smith Jr. at Red Lake (Tonalea), Arizona.[11] Judging from some contemporary newspaper accounts, the sites had been lost to Mormon memory and LDS Church researchers depended on J. P. O'Farrell, a trader at Tonalea, who found "an aged Navajo woman, Beli B'ma," who allegedly remembered the site "where Smith was treacherously slain."[12]

While the Red Lake monument site could easily match the contemporary accounts of the place where the body was abandoned, the church officials at the time believed, erroneously, that the shooting had occurred nearby. However, numerous contemporary accounts place the shooting about eleven miles away in Blue Canyon, near a dependable water source known as Buffalo Creek, Buffalo Spring, Buffalo Land, Kootsen Tooweep/Kweechum Tiveep/Quichen Too Weep/Quichintoweep, and other corruptions of Southern Paiute *quttcu* ('buffalo', 'cow') + *tïvi-ppï* ('earth,' 'ground,' 'country').[13]

APPENDIX B

Hopi People and Legends

B.1. Kuyngwu

An Orayvi named Kuringwa is mentioned a number of times by Thales Haskell; he was apparently a good friend and supporter of the missionaries and no other Hopi except Tuuvi is referred to by a Hopi name. The name is consistently spelled in full as 𐐊𐑅𐑇𐐮𐐲𐐼 (/kuiŋwɒ/) in Haskell's original Deseret Alphabet journal. At a later date, Haskell copied the Deseret Alphabet text into more or less standard English orthography and consistently spelled the name with an added *r* as Kuringwa or, shortened, Kur or "Old Kur." However, Haskell's ornate cursive *K* was confused as various letters and letter sequences in the Brigham Young University transcription,[1] and Brooks mistranscribed it as *Th*, producing Thuringwa, Thur and Old Thur, which are phonologically impossible in Hopi.[2]

After author Beesley corrected the *Th* transcriptions to *K*, Peter M. Whiteley in a personal communication identified the man as Kuyngwu (Paa'iswungwa, Desert Fox Clan, described by Mischa Titiev as the Water Coyote Clan[3]), and kindly directed our attention to Titiev's list of the nineteenth-century succession of chiefs in Orayvi with the following approximate dates:

1. Nakwayamtiwa (Nakwaiyamptiwa, Bear Clan), also known as Qötstaqa (Qötctaka, meaning "white man" because he was an albino), 1850? to 1865?;

2. Kuyngwu (Kuyingwu, Desert Fox/Water Coyote Clan), regent or "active Village chief," 1865? to "about 1880"; and

3. Loololma, recognized as chief by 1880.[4]

When Nakwayamtiwa died, the heirs apparent were the brothers Sakwhongiwma (Sakhongyoma) and Loololma (Lololoma), both of the Bear Clan; but since they were young boys, their father, Kuyngwu, was appointed as regent/acting village chief and Soyalmongwi, the chief of the important Soyal ceremony.

The Mormon missionary record helps to refine these dates. To begin with, the nineteenth-century Mormons thought that the Hopi might be "white Indians," perhaps with some white Nephite blood (harking back to the Book of Mormon story), or, perhaps more likely, Welsh blood. They were well aware of the legend of Madoc (or Madog) ab Owain Gwynedd, a Welsh prince who sailed to America in 1170, and they were actively on the lookout for a "remnant" of a Welsh tribe.[5]

Even in 1849, when Mormon apostle Parley P. Pratt, brother of Orson Pratt, led a wagon tour through Utah territory looking for possible settlement sites, there are several references to the search for a Welsh remnant.[6] The party even took along a Welshman, Dan Jones, so that he could talk to them.[7]

In 1858, when Jacob Hamblin first led missionaries to the Hopi, he also took along a Welshman, James Davis, to test the Hopi language for Welshness.[8] Another reason for this mission was, allegedly, to search for white children survivors of the Mountain Meadows Massacre (1857), who might have been living with the Hopi. The trip was at least partially funded with government money because of this search for missing white children. Some have questioned the sincerity of such a search, but a letter from Hamblin to Brigham Young appears to show that Hamblin was indeed looking for white children and apparently found one, but not from the Mountain Meadows Massacre, in Musangnuvi.[9]

In all ways, the Mormon missionaries of 1858 were actively looking for any signs of Welsh or other white influence. They visited Orayvi and were entertained there, and it is inconceivable that they would have failed to notice and record seeing an albino chief. That means that Nakwayamtiwa/Qötstaqa was already dead by late 1858 when the Mormons first arrived.

In 1859–60, when Marion Shelton and Thales Haskell spent four months in Orayvi, Haskell mentions Kuyngwu (Kuringwa) several times and indicates that he was their principal friend and helper. They would certainly have commented if the Orayvi chief at that time had been "white." However, Haskell did record, on Sunday, February 19, 1860, "Learned today that the Oribes 6 years ago used to have a White Chief of their own tribe. They speak of him as being a very good man."[10] If that is indeed a reference to Nakwayamtiwa/Qötstaqa, which seems highly likely, then he would have died about 1854, not 1865 as Titiev estimated.

B.2. Pahaana

When Hamblin first visited Orayvi in 1858, he wrote that the Hopis debated whether the missionaries were the prophesied Pahaana.[11] Of this prophecy, Whiteley writes,

> An important . . . prophecy concerns the return to Hopi of the elder white brother, Pahaana. After emergence into the present fourth world, Pahaana had departed for the east, agreeing to return at some future point to share

his acquired knowledge with the Hopi and to adjudicate between those who had sincerely adhered to the Hopi way and those who had departed from it.[12]

As the prophecy is recounted by Hamblin and Shelton,[13] the Pahaana would, as the Mormon missionaries did, return to Hopi from the *west*; all other accounts of the prophecy indicate that Pahaana would return from the *east*.[14]

In *The Invention of Prophecy: Continuity and Meaning in Hopi Indian Religion*, Armin W. Geertz examines the Pahaana prophecy in detail:

> The Hopis have been waiting for centuries, first accepting and then rejecting one White group after another as the White Brother. Some Hopis are convinced that the Americans are the White Brother and that the new era has already begun. Others reject the idea and find more meaning in clinging to the eschatological hopes and dreams.[15]

According to Geertz, the candidates considered—temporarily and by few Hopi—to be possible Pahaanas have included Jacob Hamblin, Mennonite missionary H.R. Voth, a Chinese Buddhist priest, the Bureau of Indian Affairs, U.S. soldiers, and Adolf Hitler.[16]

Format of the 1860 English-Hopi Vocabulary

The Deseret Alphabet and Hopi

The 1860 English-Hopi vocabulary was written completely in the Deseret Alphabet, which was a phonemic orthography intended originally for writing English. Despite the belief of Parley P. Pratt, Marion J. Shelton, and others that it could be used to write most other languages as a kind of international phonetic alphabet, it was hardly the ideal medium for transcribing Hopi, which has some phonemes that do not occur in English. However, because each Deseret Alphabet letter corresponds straightforwardly to a known English phoneme, the transcription of Hopi words in Deseret Alphabet is much more likely to be useful than one using only the standard twenty-six Roman letters, which have ambiguous phonemic values in traditional English orthography.

Syllabification

The Hopi words in the vocabulary are divided into syllables using periods or hyphens. While the writer sometimes uses periods and other times what appear to be raised periods or hyphens, the difference is probably not significant. Sometimes the separators are

hard to see or ambiguous, but the Deseret Alphabet letters themselves are carefully drawn and almost always clear. Although these
periods or hyphens sometimes indicate incorrect syllabification, at
other times they correspond to semivowels or glottal stops and have
been reproduced as faithfully as possible in case they prove relevant.
For example, the word <sowi> ('jackrabbit' or 'hare') is transcribed
as 𐐔𐐬.𐐨 (/ʃo.i/), and <suyan> ('easily discernible') is transcribed as
𐐔.𐐬.𐐋𐐷 (/ʃ.u.æn/).

Spelling Errors

In the vocabulary, Shelton, or another clerk, made a few spelling
errors common to Deseret Alphabet writers. The English word written
𐐪𐐆𐐭 (/mʌd/ = <mud>) in entry 467 was clearly intended to be
𐐪𐐆𐐔 (/mʌʃ/ = <mush>), as shown by the Hopi gloss 𐐸𐐪𐑉𐐲𐑅𐐰𐐿𐐨
(/hʌrusʌki/), which is <hurusuki> ('blue corn flour mush'). Note
that the /d/ letter 𐐆 is roughly a mirror image of the /ʃ/ letter 𐐔.
Similarly, writers often confuse 𐐊 (/k/) and 𐐌 (/g/), for example,
in entry 207, where the clerk clearly wrote 𐐊𐐬𐐙 (/kot/ = <coat>)
when he intended 𐐌𐐬𐐙 (/got/ = <goat>), as shown by the Hopi
gloss 𐐊𐐲.𐐮𐐬.𐑉𐐲 (/kæ.pi.rʌ/ = <kapiira>). Such scribal errors are
pointed out in individual entries where they occur.

Entry Format

The 1860 English-Hopi vocabulary, in its entirety, is reproduced in
the next section. Only the words shown in the Deseret Alphabet
appear in the original manuscript, and we have added transcriptions
in equivalent phonemic IPA and traditional English orthography
and Hopi orthography from modern dictionaries. The modern Hopi
words and spellings cited from Milo Kalectaca's vocabulary of
Second-Mesa Hopi are marked **MK**, those from Seaman's dictionary

as **SE**, and those found in the authoritative *Hopi Dictionary—Hopìikwa Lavàytutuveni* are marked **HD**.[1] For example, where the original vocabulary entry is just the two words

ℰ⅃Ѳ, ⅂Ә.Ѳ

it is expanded in the reproduction to

boy /bɔʲ/ ℰ⅃Ѳ — ⅂Ә.Ѳ /ti.o/, HD p. 598 *tiyo*; MK p. 216 *tiyo*.

We have tried to represent the vocabulary content as faithfully as possible and in the original order. The letter-labeled sections generally appear in the alphabetic order implied in standard Deseret Alphabet charts, but there is a slight digression in the vowels. In the standard charts, as shown in Figure 2.2 on page 13, the long vowels are all ordered before the short vowels. In the English-Hopi vocabulary, the long Ә (/i/) and short ⸆ (/ɪ/) entries are grouped together, followed by the long Ʒ (/e/) and short ⅃ (/ɛ/) entries, etc. Letter labels were repeated at the tops of new pages, and these repetitions have been retained. The document ends with a section of "miscellaneous," mostly closed-class words, which include pronouns, *yes*, *no*, *here*, *there*, and various other function words. A few duplicate entries and a crossed-out entry are reproduced from the original. As previously stated, the manuscript is carefully written with very few corrections and may well be a fair copy of the original field notes by some clerk other than Shelton.

Inside each section, the entries are presented in the original unalphabetized order, which sometimes suggests a semantic thread followed during original collection. We have added numbering of the entries and an index of English words in standard alphabetical order to facilitate referencing.

Text of the 1860 English-Hopi Vocabulary

𐐀. 𐐆. — i. ɪ.

1. **ear** /ir/ 𐐨𐐡 — 𐐤𐐲𐐿.𐐲.𐑂𐐳. /nʌk.ʌ.vʊ./, HD p. 303 *naqvu*

2. **eat** /it/ 𐐨𐐻 — 𐐻𐐮𐑋.𐐳.𐐮𐐻. /tɪm.ʊ.ɪt./, HD p. 685 *tuumoyta* ‘be eating’; MK p. 219 *tuumoyta*

3. **evening** /ivnŋ/ 𐐨𐑂𐑌𐑍 — 𐐻𐐪.𐑇𐐲𐐹.𐐻𐐰. /tɑ.ʃʌp.tæ./, HD p. 564 *taasupi* ‘twilight, the yellow-reddish twilight noticeable along the western sky after the sun has set’; SE p. 83 *taasupi* ‘evening red in the sky’; Probably *taasapti*, a derived verbal form of *taasupi*, meaning ‘become evening’; or plausibly *?taasapta* or *?taasupta*, a previously unattested form that would mean ‘make it to evening.’

4. **image** /ɪmɛʤ/ 𐐮𐑋𐐯𐑅 — 𐐻𐐨.𐐸𐐲. /ti.hʌ./, HD p. 591 *tihu* ‘child’; *tithu* ‘kachina doll’; MK p. 218 *tihu* ‘doll’; “Image” is almost certainly intended by Shelton in the sense of idol or “graven image.” Haskell writes, “Went into one place where they were making and painting little wooden images about 6 inches long.”[1] Also, “Indians making images and other tringets [trinkets] for a big performance.”[2]

5. **enough** /inʌf/ 𐐨𐑌𐐲𐑁 — 𐐹𐐬.𐑇𐑌. /po.ʃn./, HD p. 372 *pàasa’* (*paus.* pàasa’a) ‘that’s enough, that’s all, it’s all gone’; This is the only plausible guess. The discrepancies in

transcription might result from a clerk's copying errors, especially here near the beginning of the vocabulary. In particular, the glyph 𐐴, here transliterated as /n/, represented /æ/ in an earlier version of the Deseret Alphabet.

6. **increase** /ɪnkris/ 𐐻𐐲𐐼𐐮𐑇 — 𐐤𐐲.𐐬𐐶𐐾𐐲.𐑀𐐬.𐑂𐐬.𐑂𐐬.𐐻𐐴. /nɑ.kwʊm.ho.jo.jo.tn./, HD pp. 339, 107 *nukwangwhoyoyota* 'be growing nicely,' from *nukwangw-* (fem. spkr.) 'good,' and *hoyoyota* 'to be moving along, be moving in a specified direction, progressing' or 'for plants to grow'; The lip-rounded velar nasal written <ngw> is acoustically similar to the /m/ apparently heard by Shelton. The final /n/ is probably a copyist's error, see the comment in entry 5.

7. **enclose** /ɪnkloz/ 𐐻𐐲𐐬𐌾𐐬𐑇 — 𐑄𐐬.𐐬𐑂𐐾.𐐴𐐻. /mo.kjæ.tʌ./, HD p. 243 *mokyàa|ta* 'wrap up, bag something'

8. **irrigate** /ɪrɪget/ 𐐮𐑉𐐮𐑀𐐩𐐻 — 𐑄𐑀𐐮𐐴.𐌾𐐬.𐌾𐐾.𐐴𐐻. /mʊɪn.lɑ.la^j.tʌ./, HD pp. 260–61 *munlalay|to* 'go

to channel flood water, irrigate'

3. ᴵ. — e. ε.

9. **elbow** /ɛlbo/ 𐐴𐌾𐐯𐐬 — 𐐕𐐾.𐐯𐐻.𐐾𐌾. /tʃɛ.vɪ.æt./, HD p. 649 *tsövi('at)*

10. **egg** /ɛg/ 𐐾𐐰 — 𐐴𐐬.𐑁𐑅 /ni.hʊ/, HD p. 331 *nöhu*; MK p. 219 *nöhu*

ᴼ. ᴵ — ɑ. æ

11. **arm** /ɑrm/ 𐐩𐑁𐐬 — 𐑅𐐰.𐐾𐐻 /mɑ.æt/, HD p. 217 *maa('at)* 'arm' (body part)

12. **ask** /ɑsk/ 𐐯𐑅𐐰 — 𐑇-𐐯𐐻𐑋-𐐴𐑉 /te-bɪŋ-tʌ/, HD p. 692 *tuuving|ta* 'ask, inquire of'; MK p. 214 *tuuvingta*

13. **axe** /æks/ 𐌾𐐰𐑅 — 𐑇𐐰.𐐬𐑂𐌾.𐐴.𐐶𐌾. /pi.kjæ.ŋ.wʊ./, HD p. 412 *pikya'yngwa*

14. **assistant chiefs** /æsɪstænt-tʃifs/ 𐌾𐑅𐐻𐑅𐌾𐐴𐐻-𐐕𐐲𐐒𐑅 — 𐑇𐐬𐐤.𐐒𐐻𐐴.𐐶𐌾.𐐬𐌾𐐴.𐑉 /moŋ.ʃɪŋ.wʊ.mæt.ʌ/, HD p. 246 *mongsungwa('at)* 'one's chief partner, fellow chief'

15. **ashes** /æʃez/ 𐌾𐐗𐐲𐑅 — 𐐬𐑉.𐑉.𐐕𐐻.𐐯𐐬. /kʌ.ʌ.tʃɪ.vi./, HD p. 479 *qötsvi* 'ash, ashes'

16. **ash (timber)** /æʃ (tɪmbr)/

ᒍᗃ (ꞟ⊦Ɔ8⊦) — ꝺШ⊦Ⴈ.Ɔ.Ᏺ⊦.
/kwɪŋ.o.bɪ./, HD p. 184 *kwingvi* 'scrub oak'

17. **antelope** /æntɪlop/ ᒍᴎꞟ⊦ᒐᏅꞟ — ᏟᎧ.Ᏺ⊦.ᏲᏅ. /tʃi.vɪ.jo./, HD p. 646 *tsööviw* 'pronghorn antelope'

18. **arrive** /æraʲv/ ᒍ⊦ᒑᏸ — ꞟᎧ.ꞟ⊦. /pi.tɪ./, HD p. 418 *pitu* (sg.), *öki* (pl.); MK p. 202 *pitu, öki* (pl.)

Ꝺ. ᒑ. — Ɔ. ᗞ.

19. **all** /ɔl/ Ᏺᒐ — ᗞɔ.ᗞɔꝺ /ʃo.ʃok/, HD p. 521 *sòosok* 'all, everything'

20. **almost** /ɔl-most/ Ᏺᒐ-ᏆᏫ8ꞟ — ꝺᎧ.ꝺ⊦ᴎ /hi.hɪn/, HD p. 69 *hihin* 'barely'

21. **ox** /ɒks/ ᒑᏫ8 — ШᒑꝺᏫ.ᒑ8 /wɒk.ɒs/, HD p. 725 *waakasi* 'cow, bovine of either sex'; From Spanish *vaca*.

22. **oxhide** /ɒkshaʲd/ ᒑᏫ8ꞟᒑᏋ — ШᒑꝺᏫ.ᒑᗞ⊦.ᏟᎧᏫ.Ꮙᒑ /wɒk.ɒʃɪ.vʊk.jæ/, HD pp. 725, 450 *waakasi* 'cow, bovine animal of either sex' + -*vukya*, (*comb.* of *puukya*) 'skin, animal hide'

Ꝺ. ᒐ — o. ᴧ

23. **old** /old/ ᏲᒐᎧ — Шᒑ.ᏉᎤ.ꞟᒐ /wʌ.jo.tʌ/, HD p. 764 *wuyòoti* 'become old, age'

24. **old man** /old-mæn/ ᏲᒐᎧ-Ɔᒍᴎ — ШᏀᏉ.ꞟᒐᏫ.ᒐ /wʊh.tʌk.ʌ/, HD p. 756 *wùutaqa* 'old man'

25. **old woman** /old-wʊmæn/ ᏲᒐᎧ-ШᏀᏆᒍᴎ — ШᏀᏉ.ꞟ⊦.ꞟᒐ8.ꝺᒐ /wʊh.tɪ.hʌs.kʌ/, HD p. 757 *wùutiharku* 'ripe old woman, very old woman'

26. **open** /opn/ Ꮖᴎ — ꞟ3.Ꮯ⊦ /he.tʃɪ/, HD p. 111 *hötsi* 'opening, open space, gap'

27. **earth** /ʌrθ/ ᒐꞟᒐ — ꞟᏋᏟ.ꝺᏆᎧ.Ᏺᒐ /tetʃ.kwa.vʌ/, HD pp. 678, 816 *tutskwa(ve(q))* 'land, ground, earth, soil'

28. **ugly** /ʌglɪ/ ᒐᏯᒐ⊦ — ꝺᒐ.ᗞᏯ.Ꭴ⊦.Шᒑ /kʌ.ʃo.nɪ.wɒ/, HD p. 520 *qa sóniw|a* (lit: 'not pretty')

29. **understand** /ʌndrstænd/ ᒐᎤᏯ⊦8ᒍᏯᏋ — ꞟ3.ᏆᒑᎾ /te.kaʲt/, HD p. 672 *tuqayi'y|ta* 'have heard'

Ш. — w.

30. **wood** /wʊd/ ШᏀᏋ — ꝺᏫ.ꞟᏫ /ko.ho/, HD p. 145 *koho* [Third Mesa]; MK p. 234 *kwuhu*

[Second Mesa]

31. **woman** /wʊmæn/ ꭰꭲꝺꝵ — ꭹꝼꝼ.ꞁꞁ /wʊh.tɪ/, HD p. 757 *wùuti* (sg.); MK p. 234 *wuùti*, *momoyam* (pl.); In the Second-Mesa Musangnuvi dialect (2MM), the word is <wuhti>.

32. **wool** /wʊl/ ꭰꝼꞁ — ꞁꞁ.ꝼꞁꝼ /pɪ.hɪh/, HD p. 436 *pöhö* 'fur, body hair, wool, fleece'

33. **wolf** /wʊlf/ ꭰꝼꞁꝼ — ꞁꝺ.ꞌꝰ.ꭰꞃ /iʃ.aʷ.wʌ/, HD p. 123 *iisaw* 'coyote'; MK p. 217 *iisaw*

34. **window** /wɪndo/ ꭰꞁꝷꞌꞁꝺꝺ — ꞁꝺꝺ.ꝺꞁ /pok.ʃɪ/, HD p. 420 *poksö* 'ventilating hole, window'

35. **water** /wɔtr/ ꭰꝼꞁꝼ — ꝺꝼ.ꞁ /kʊ.ɪ/, HD p. 162 *kuuyi*; MK p. 233 *kuuyi*

36. **water vessel** /wɔtr-vɛsl/ ꭰꝼꞁꝼ-ꞃꝷꞁꞁ — ꭰꝺ.ꝺꝺ.ꝼꞃ /wi.ko.rʌ/, HD pp. 858, 736 *wikoro* 'water jug,' 'bottle, jug or vase with a narrow neck or small spout, jar, canteen'

37. **wet** /wɛt/ ꭰꝵꞁ — ꝼꝷ.ꞁꝷ.ꝺꞃ /hæ.læ.ʃʌ/, HD pp. 57, 833 *halasam'iw|ta* 'be moistened, wet (of ground)'; *halasami* 'moist ground'

38. **weak** /wik/ ꭰꝵꝺ — ꝵꞁꝺ.ꝺꝵ.ꝷꞃ /nʌk.ʃi.vʌ/, HD p. 338 *nuksiwa* 'spineless one, one lacking fortitude, coward'

ꭰ. — w.

39. **wind** /wɪnd/ ꭰꞁꝵꝵꝵ — ꝼꞃ.ꝼꞃꞁ.ꝺꝵꝷ /hʌ.hʌɪ.kjæ./, HD p. 117 *huuhuk|ya* 'for the wind to be blowing, gusting'

40. **warm** /wɔrm/ ꭰꝵꞁꝺ — ꞁ.ꞁꞁ.ꝼ.ꞁ.ꞁ /i.tɪ.h.ɪ.ɪ/, HD p. 715 *utuhu'u* (weather) 'hot'

41. **worn** /worn/ ꭰꝺꞁꝵ — ꝺꝵꝺ.ꭰꝵꞁ /ʃæk.wit/, HD p. 490 *sakwi* 'worn out, broken down, dilapidated, in disrepair, ruined'

42. **weave** /wiv/ ꭰꝵꞌ — ꞁꞃ.ꝺꞁꝵ.ꞁꞃ /pe.kʌn.tʌ/, HD p. 440 *pööqan|ta* 'be weaving'

43. **walk** /wɔk/ ꭰꝵꝺ — ꭰꞁ.ꝵꝷ.ꝺꞃ /waʲ.ni.mʌ/, HD p. 731 *waynum|a* 'be walking around'; MK p. 210 *wayma*

44. **wash hands** /waʃ-hændz/ ꭰꝵꝺ-ꝼꝵꝵꞌꝵ — ꝺꝵ.ꝵꝵꝷ.ꞃ.ꞁꞁ /ma.vɒk.ʌ.tɪ/, HD p. 222 *maavaq|ta* 'wash the hands'

45. **wash face** /" fes/ " ꞁꝵꞁ — ꞁꝺ.ꝺꝷ.ꝵꝵ.ꝵꝵꞌꝷ.ꞃ.ꞁꞁ /po.ʃi.mɒ.vɒk.ʌ.tɪ/, HD p. 430

posimavaq|ta 'wash the face';
The double quotes in this and
the next three entries denote
"ditto," referring to the word
wash in the previous entry.

46. wash clothes /" kloz/ "
ⵀⵍⵓ6 — ꓩ3.ꛗꝛ.ꝼꝋ.ꝋꝛ
/te.bʌ.ho.mʌ/, HD p. 691
tuuvahom|a 'wash, launder'

47. wash body /" bɒdɪ/ "
ꛒꝡꝋꝷ — ꜘꝋ.Ꝺꝛ.ꝼꝋ.ꝋꝛ
/na.vʌ.ho.mʌ/, HD p. 283
naavahoma 'take a bath, bathe
oneself'

48. wash head /" hɛd/ " ꝼꝯꝋ
— Ꝺꝋ /aʃ/, HD p. 12 *aasi* 'wash
the hair'; MK p. 233 *aasi* 'wash
hair'

49. willow /wɪlo/ ꙡꝷⵀⵀ —
ꝋꝛ.ꝼꝋ.Ꝺꝷ /kʌ.ha.bɪ/, HD p. 458
qahavi 'willow'

50. wildcat /waʲld-kæt/
ꙡꝷⵍꝋ-ꝋꝯꝷ — ꝷꝋ.ꝋꝋ.Ꝺꝷ /to.ko.tʃɪ/,
HD p. 600 *tokotsi*

51. watermelon /wɔtr-mɛln/
ꙡꝋꝷꝷ-ꝋꝷⵍꜚ — ꝋꝰꝰ.Ꝗ.ꝼꝛ.ꝯꝰ.ꝯꝛꜚ
/kav.aʲ.jʌ.væ.tʌŋ/, HD p. 137
kawayvatnga; MK p. 233
kawayvatnga

52. will /wɪl/ ꙡꝷⵀ — ꝺꝋꝷ.ꝋꝰ
/ʃon.kɑ/, HD p. 519 *son qa*

'necessarily, surely, inevitably,
always, must, undoubtedly,
probably, can (be able to), it
must be'

53. will not /wɪl-nɒt/ ꙡꝷⵀ-ꜘꝯꝷ
— ꝺꝋꜚ /ʃon/, HD pp. 519, 515
so'on, son. so'on|i "will not" [i.e.,
"I don't want to"]

54. want /wɔnt/ ꙡꝋꜚꝷ —
ꜘꝯ.ꝛ.ꙡꝯꝋ.ꝷꜚ /naʲ.ʌ.wɒk.ɪn/, HD p.
284 *naawakna* 'want, desire';
MK p. 199 *naawakna*

55. wind /waʲnd/ ꙡꝯꜚꝋ —
ꓩ3.ⵀ3.ꙡꜚꜚ.ꝷꝛ /pe.le.læn.tʌ/, HD p.
438 *pölölan|ta* 'be making into a
ball'

ꝼ. — j.

56. young man /jʌŋmæn/
ꝭꝛꜚꝺꙡꜚ — ꝺꝰꝷ.ꝼ3.ⵀꝯꝷ
/ʃʊp.he.laʷt/, HD p. 542
suphelaw|ta 'be in the original or
pristine state'; This might mean
"pristine state" in the sense of
virgin. See entry 381, where the
same word is used to gloss *maid.*

57. year /jir/ ꝭꝯꝷ — ꝭꝯ.ꝺꝯꜚ.ꝋꝰꝾꝾ
/jæ.ʃæŋ.vʊ/, HD p. 768
yàasangw

ꝼ. — h.

58. horse /hɒrs/ ꝼꙡꝷ8 —

𐐿𐐲.𐑂𐐴.𐐷𐐲 /kʌ.vaʲ.jʌ/, HD p. 136 *kaway|o*; MK p. 222 *kawayo*

59. **wheat** /hwit/ 𐐸𐐶𐐨𐐻 — 𐑇𐐲.𐐸𐐩.𐑂𐐳.𐑇𐐮 /ʃʌ.he.vʊ.ʃɪ/, HD p. 527 *söhövosi*

60. **hare** /her/ 𐐸𐐩𐑉 — 𐑇𐐬.𐐨 /ʃo.i/, HD p. 525 *sow|i* 'jackrabbit'

61. **hammer** /hæmr/ 𐐸𐐰𐑋𐑉 — 𐐻𐐰.𐐹𐐲𐑋.𐐹𐐨 /tæ.pʌm.pi/, HD p. 576 *tapàmpi*

62. **harvest** /hɑrvɛst/ 𐐸𐐪𐑉𐑂𐐯𐑅𐐻 — 𐐸𐐩.𐐸𐐩.𐐱𐐿.𐐲.𐐷𐐰 /he.he.ɒk.ʌ.jæ/, HD p. 108 *höhöq|ö(~ya)* 'be harvesting'

63. **heavy** /hɛvɪ/ 𐐸𐐯𐑂𐐮 — 𐐹𐐳𐐻 /pʊt/, HD p. 449 *putu* 'heavy, burdensome'

64. **hurricane** /hʌrɪken/ 𐐸𐐲𐑉𐐮𐐿𐐩𐑌 — 𐐿𐐲.𐐮.𐐷𐐰𐑌.𐐹𐐬.𐐹𐐬𐐻 /kʌ.ɪ.jæn.po.pot/, HD p. 470 *qö'angwpopota* 'for dust to be repeatedly raised up,' from *qö'angw* 'dust raised by the wind' and *opopota* 'to be filling up repeatedly.' See also the related forms *qö'àngwpokin|ta*, *qö'àngwpokiw|ta* 'for dust to be raised up,' *qö'àngwpokna*, *qö'àngwpokni'y|ma*, *qö'àngwpokni'ynum|a*, *qö'àngwpokni'y|ta*

65. **high** /haʲ/ 𐐸𐐴 — 𐐸𐐩.𐐮 /he.ɪ/, HD p. 108 *hö'i* 'deep'; SE p. 22 *hœ'i* 'deep, high, hollow'

66. **hole** /hol/ 𐐸𐐬𐑊 — 𐐹𐐬.𐑉𐐬𐐿.𐐹𐐳 /po.rok.pʊ/, HD pp. 825, 429 *pórokpu* 'open ended hole or perforation'

67. **hill** /hɪl/ 𐐸𐐮𐑊 — 𐐽𐐬.𐑋𐐬 /ʧo.mo/, HD p. 638 *tsomo*; MK p. 93 *tsomo*

𐐸. — h.

68. **housewifery** /haʷswaʲfrɪ/ 𐐸𐐵𐑅𐐶𐐴𐑁𐑉𐐮 — 𐐻𐐩.𐑊𐐩.𐐬.𐐿𐐲.𐐷𐐰 /te.le.o.kʌ.jæ/, HD p. 685 *tuulewkya* 'weaver'

69. **husband** /hʌzbænd/ 𐐸𐐲𐑆𐐺𐐰𐑌𐐼 — 𐐹𐐳𐐮.𐐶𐐮𐑇.𐐮𐑍.𐐶𐐴𐐻 /pʊɪ.wɪʃ.ɪŋ.waʲt/, HD p. 453 *puwsungw|a('at)* 'husband'; *-at* third-person possessive

70. **happy** /hæpɪ/ 𐐸𐐰𐐹𐐮 — 𐐻𐐴.𐐷𐐰𐐻.𐐴 /taʲ.jæt.aʲ/, HD p. 589 *tayati* 'laugh'

71. **hungry** /hʌŋgrɪ/ 𐐸𐐲𐑍𐑀𐑉𐐮 — 𐐽𐐱𐑍.𐐮𐑋𐐬.𐐿𐐮 /ʧɒŋ.ɪmo.kɪ/, HD p. 644 *tsöngmok|i(~ya)* 'get hungry (for)'

72. **hunt** /hʌnt/ 𐐸𐐲𐑌𐐻 — 𐐸𐐯𐐹.𐐻𐐬 /hɛp.to/, HD p. 68 *hep|to* 'go to

seek, look for'; MK p. 192 *hevto* 'go look for'

73. **hang** /hæŋ/ 𐐙𐐒𐐜 — 𐐙.𐑅.𐐜 /haʲ.jʲu.tʌ/, HD p. 54 *haayiw|ta* 'be hanging'

74. **hit** /hɪt/ 𐐙𐐡 — 𐐃𐑀.𐐒𐑄 /mʌp.ʃɪ/, HD p. 230 *mapsi* 'good shooter, one who throws or shoots with accuracy'

75. **have** /hæv/ 𐐙𐐜𐐒 — 𐐒𐐃.𐐔.𐐒𐑄 /kuʃ.i.vʌ/, HD p. 189 *kwusiva* 'bring'

76. **hurt** /hrt/ 𐐙𐐡 — 𐑄-3-𐑄.𐐒𐑄 /t-e-ɪ.vʌŋ/, HD p. 702 *tuyvana(~ya)* 'start to have pain from a natural cause, esp. labor pains'

77. **whip** /hwɪp/ 𐐙𐐒𐐡 — 𐐒𐐒𐐔-𐑄𐑀 /wuv-a-tʌ/, HD p. 760 *wuvàa|ta* 'hit, whip, lash, deliver a blow, strike'

78. **herd** /hrd/ 𐐙𐐔𐐒 — 𐐒𐐒𐐒-𐑄-𐑄𐑀 /lal-aʲ-tʌ/, HD p. 197 *laalay|to* 'go to herd'

79. **head** /hɛd/ 𐐙𐐒𐐒 — 𐐒𐑄-𐐡𐑄-3-𐐜 /kʌ-ʌt-e-æt/, HD p. 477 *qötö('at)* (anat.) 'head'; MK p. 222 *qötö*

80. **hand** /hænd/ 𐐙𐐒𐐒𐐒 — 𐐃𐑄-𐑄-𐑄𐑀 /mʌk-ʌ-tu/, HD p. 231 *maqtö* 'back of the hand'

81. **heart** /hart/ 𐐙𐐒𐐡𐑄 — 𐑄-𐐡𐑄-𐐒𐐒 /ɪn-ʌŋ-wɒ/, HD p. 708 *unangw|a*

82. **hip** /hɪp/ 𐐙𐐡𐑄 — 𐐙𐐒-𐐒𐑄-𐐒𐑄 /ho-vɪ-æt/, HD p. 99 *hoovi('at)* 'area of the buttocks'

83. **hook** /huk/ 𐐙𐐒𐐒 — 𐐒𐐒𐐒𐐒-3-𐑄𐐒-𐐒𐑄 /ŋwɛl-e-to-ɒŋ/, HD pp. 825, 319 *ngölöwtangwu*, from *ngölöw|ta* 'be looped or bent' with the habitual ending *-ngwu*.

84. **hot** /hɒt/ 𐐙𐐒𐐡 — 𐐃𐑄-𐐡𐐒-𐑄 /mʌ-ʌk-ɪ/, HD p. 258 *muki* 'warm'; MK p. 198 *muki* 'hot'

85. **hat** /hæt/ 𐐙𐐒𐐡 — 𐑄𐐒-𐑄𐐒𐐒-𐐡𐐒-𐐡-𐐒𐑄 /pi-tæn-ʌk-ʌ-tʃɪ/, HD p. 416 *pitanaktsi*; MK p. 202 *pitanaktsi*

ꓶ. — p.

86. **plate** /plet/ 𐐜𐐒𐑄𐑄 — 𐐒𐐒.𐐒𐐡𐑄.𐑄𐑀 /tʃa.kap.tʌ/, HD p. 622 *tsaqapta* 'pottery bowl, earthenware, dish or bowl, plate, pan'

87. **peaches** /pitʃɛz/ 𐑄𐐒𐐒𐐒 — 𐑄𐑄.𐑄𐐒.𐐒𐑄 /sɪ.pa.lʌ/, HD p. 505 *sipala* 'peach'; MK p. 205 *sipala*

88. **pumpkin** /pʌmpkɪn/ 𐑄𐐒𐐒𐐒𐐒𐐡𐑄 — 𐑄𐐒-𐑄𐐡𐑄-𐐒 /pa-tʌŋ-æ/,

HD p. 396 *patnga* 'squash, pumpkin, cucurbit'; MK p. 228 *patnga*

89. **pole** /pol/ 𐐓𐐬𐑊 — 𐐢𐐱𐐜-𐐻𐐯𐐰-𐐻 /leʃ-tab-ɪ/, HD p. 207 *lestavi* 'beam, main roof timber'

90. **paper** /pepr/ 𐐓𐐯𐐓𐑉 — 𐐻𐐻.𐐻𐐻.𐐰𐑇𐑇.𐐔𐐻.𐐢𐑉𐐩.𐐻.𐐢3 /tɪ.tɪ.bɪn.ʃɪ.lʌk.ɪ.we/, HD pp. 681, 502 *tutuveni* 'visual or written representation or symbol,' *silaqvu* 'cornhusk(s)'

91. **potatoes** /potetoz/ 𐐓𐐬𐐓3𐐓𐐬6 — 𐐻𐐻𐐬.𐑅𐐻 /tɪm.nɪ/, HD p. 665 *tumna*; MK p. 228 *tumna*

92. **panther** /pænθr/ 𐐓𐐩𐑄𐐢𐐻 — 𐐓𐐬.𐑃𐐬 /to.ho/, HD p. 599 *tohòo* (*var.* toho, tohow) 'mountain lion'; MK p. 224 *toho* 'leopard'; In his journal entry for 26 January 1860, Thales Haskell wrote, "Took breakfast with br Shelton at his lodgings had corn bread and soup made from the meat of a panther."[3]

93. **pipe** /paʲp/ 𐐓𐐶𐑁 — 𐐗𐐬𐑇.𐐬 /tʃoŋ.o/, HD p. 640 *tsoongo* 'smoking pipe'; MK p. 227 *tsoongo*

94. **pipe-stem** /paʲp-stɛm/ 𐐓𐐶𐑁-𐑅𐑄𐐬 — 𐑄𐐬.𐑄𐐬.𐑃𐐬.𐑄𐑁

/mo.mo.pi.æt/, HD p. 245 *momòypi* 'mouthpiece'

95. **people** /pipl/ 𐐓𐐬𐑉𐑊 — 𐐔𐐰.𐑅𐐬𐑇 /ʃi.nom/, HD p. 504 *sinom* (acc. pl. of *sin|o* 'person'); MK p. 205 *sino* 'person'

96. **provisions** /prʌvɪʒʌnz/ 𐐓𐑁𐑉𐐶𐑇𐑅𐑉𐑇6 — 𐑄𐐬.𐐷𐐬𐑇 /no.vat/, HD p. 329 *noova* 'cooked food'

97. **pretty** /prɪtɪ/ 𐐓𐑁𐑁𐑁𐑁 — 𐐔9.𐑁𐐬.𐐬𐑉 /ʃu.hi.mʌ/, HD p. 534 *súhimu* 'handsome, attractive one (generally of a male)'

98. **poor** /pur/ 𐐓𐐬𐑁 — 𐐬.𐐬𐐬.𐐢𐑇 /o.ki.wɒ/, HD p. 350 *oo'okiw* 'poor, destitute'; MK p. 200 *okiw* 'poor thing'

𐐙. — b.

99. **bet** /bɛt/ 𐐙𐑅𐑁 — 𐑇𐐬.𐑇𐐷𐐙.𐐻.𐑉 /na.næb.ɪ.ʌ/, HD p. 299 *nanavö'|a* 'be gambling'

100. **break** /brek/ 𐐙𐐻3𐐬 — 𐐬𐑉.𐑉.𐑃𐐬 /kʌ.ʌ.hi/, HD p. 470 *qöhi(k-)* 'for a linear segment of a (usu. rigid) object to break'

101. **broil** /brɔʲl/ 𐐙𐐻𐑄𐑊 — 𐑇𐐶𐑃.𐑄𐑉 /tʊh.pɛ/, HD pp. 686, 810 *tùupe* 'prepare food using heat,' 'cook, bake, roast'

102. **blow** /blo/ 𐐙𐑊𐐬 —

𐐰𐐹.𐐬.𐑂𐐲𐑊.𐐲 /æp.o.vʌl.ʌ/, HD p. 428 *poovoya* 'blow with the mouth'

103. **bend** /bnd/ 𐐺𐑌𐐼 — 𐑍𐐶𐐲𐑊.𐐮 /ŋwʌl.ɪ/, HD pp. 318, 319 *ngöla* 'hoop, ring (not of the finger)'; *ngöla|ta* 'make a wheel, hoop'

104. **bite** /ba^{j}t/ 𐐺𐐴𐐻 — 𐐿𐐷𐐰.𐐽𐐲𐑌𐐻.𐐲 /kjæ.tʃʌnt.ʌ/, HD p. 192 *kyàatsan|ta* 'hold in the mouth, between the teeth'

105. **brown, (verb)** /bra^{w}n, (vrb)/ 𐐺𐑉𐐵𐑌, (𐑂𐑉𐐺) — 𐐿𐐬.𐐸𐐪𐑊.𐐿𐐱𐐹.𐐲.𐐷𐐳.𐐻𐐲. /ko.hɑl.kɒp.ʌ.jʊ.tʌ./, HD p. 145 *kohàlqap'iw|ta* 'be crusty from baking or cooking'

106. **back-bone** /bæk-bon/ 𐐺𐐰𐐿-𐐺𐐬𐑌 — 𐐸𐐬𐐻.𐐰𐐻 /hot.æt/, HD pp. 103, 98 *hot|'öqa* 'backbone'; hòota('at) 'back as body part'

107. **breast** /brɛst/ 𐐺𐑉𐐯𐑅𐐻 — 𐐹𐐨.𐐸𐐨.𐐰𐐻 /pi.hi.æt/, HD p. 409 *piihu*; *-'at* third-person possessive

108. **breastbone** /brɛstbon/ 𐐺𐑉𐐯𐑅𐐻𐐺𐐬𐑌 — 𐐻𐐱.𐐶𐐮𐐽.𐐿𐐮.𐐰𐐻 /tɒ.wɪtʃ.kɪ.æt/, HD p. 587 *tawitsqa* 'breast area, chest'; *-'at* third-person possessive

109. **belly** /bɛlɪ/ 𐐺𐐯𐑊𐐮 — 𐐹𐐬.𐑌𐐬.𐐰𐐻 /po.no.æt/, HD p. 424 *pono* 'stomach, belly, waist area'; *-'at* third-person possessive

110. **hickory shirt** /hɪkʌrɪ-ʃrt/ 𐐸𐐮𐐿𐐲𐑉𐐮-𐑇𐑉𐐻 — 𐑇𐐰𐐿.𐐶𐐪-𐐿𐐶𐐨.𐐿𐐶𐐨𐑊-𐐽𐐪.𐐽𐐰𐐿.𐐲𐑋.𐐨.𐐽𐐲𐐿.𐑌𐐲𐐹.𐑌𐐪 /ʃæk.wɑ-kwi.kwil-tʃɑ.tʃæk.ʌm.i.tʃʌk.nʌp.nɑ/, HD pp. 489, 183, 623, 302 *sakwa* 'turquoise blue color or material + *kwikwil-* 'striped with several stripes' + *tsatsakwmötsapu* 'manufactured cloth, finely woven cloth, fabric of the texture that shirts and dresses are made of' + *napna* 'shirt'; Hickory shirts, heavy cotton work shirts with narrow blue and white vertical stripes, can still be purchased today and were used by some agricultural workers, train engineers, machinists and lumberjacks. See entry 225.

𐐻. — t.

111. **tighten** /ta^{j}tn/ 𐐻𐐴𐐻𐑌 — 𐑊𐐲𐑍.𐐲𐐿.𐐲𐑌 /lʌŋ.ʌk.ʌn/, HD p. 200 *lángakna(~ya)* 'pull or tug on, stretch out,' *lángakin|ta* 'be pulling on or stretching out'

112. **trap** /træp/ 𐐻𐑉𐐰𐐹 — 𐐽𐐰.𐐿𐐪𐑋.𐐲 /tʃæ.kam.ʌ/, HD p. 622 *tsaqami* ‘deadfall’; *tsaqam|a(~ya)* ‘set a deadfall’; Haskell writes, “I went with an Indian down to some cottonwood trees and made a dead fall to catch a wolf and packed home a load of wood.”[4] Later his “landlord” asked him to make another one.[5]

113. **turn** /tʌrn/ 𐐻𐐲𐑉𐑌 — 𐐿𐐲.𐑌𐐨𐑌.𐐮.𐐻𐐲 /kʌ.nin.ɪ.tʌ/, HD p. 473 *qönini|ta* ‘be whirling, reeling, turning around and around in place’

114. **tired** /taʲrd/ 𐐻𐐴𐑉𐐼 — 𐑋𐐰.𐑍𐐮 /mæ.ŋɪ/, HD pp. 219, 854, 227 *maangu’|i* ‘become tired,’ *mangu’iw* ‘tiredness, weariness’

115. **teeth** /tiθ/ 𐐻𐐨𐑃 — 𐐻𐐫𐑋.𐐲 /tɒm.ʌ/, HD p. 573 *tama* ‘tooth’; MK p. 232 *tama*

116. **tongue** /tʌŋ/ 𐐻𐐲𐑍 — 𐑊𐐩𐑌.𐐷𐐲 /len.jʌ/, HD p. 205 *lengi(’at)*; MK p. 232 *lengi*

117. **tear** /ter/ 𐐻𐐩𐑉 — 𐐽𐐨.𐐿𐐷𐐲 /tʃi.kjʌ/, HD pp. 628–29, 843 *tsiikya(~ya)* ‘divide, tear, slice’; *tsiik|i* ‘get divided, tear, rip’

𐐑. — p.

118. **poor in flesh** /pur-ɪn-flɛʃ/ 𐐹𐐭𐑉-𐐮𐑌-𐑁𐑊𐐯𐑇 — 𐑊𐐲𐐿.𐐸𐐲.𐑉𐐲 /lʌk.hʌ.rʌ/, HD pp. 198, 847 *lakharu* ‘skinny one’

119. **plenty** /plɛntɪ/ 𐐹𐑊𐐯𐑌𐐻𐐮 — 𐑌𐐨𐐸.𐐻𐐮.𐐷𐐬.𐐻𐐲 /nih.tɪ.jo.tʌ/, HD pp. 325, 838 *nìitiw|ta* ‘be many, a surplus, a lot, extra, a multitude; abound’

120. **plant** /plænt/ 𐐹𐑊𐐰𐑌𐐻 — 𐐳.𐐮.𐑊𐐵 /ʊ.ɪ.laʷ/, HD pp. 719, 838 *uy|lawu* ‘plant seeds in ground’; MK p. 227 *uuya* ‘plant’

121. **parch** /partʃ/ 𐐹𐐪𐑉𐐽 — 𐐻𐐩.𐐽𐐲 /te.tʃʌ/, HD p. 657 *tu’tsi* ‘fresh husked corn on the cob, roasted over opencoals’

122. **pass** /pæs/ 𐐹𐐰𐑅 — 𐑌𐐪.𐑇𐐵.𐑂𐐴.𐐷𐐲 /na.ʃaʷ.vaʲ.jʌ/, HD p. 280 *nàasawva(~ya)* ‘meet going opposite directions’

123. **pulverize** /pʌlvraʲz/ 𐐹𐐲𐑊𐑂𐑉𐐴𐑆 — 𐑋𐐬.𐑋𐐬𐑇.𐐻𐐲 /mo.moʃ.tʌ/, HD p. 245 Perhaps something to do with *momri* or *momsi* ‘crush, pulverize’ (as in crushing dry bean pods to get the beans out) or a gavagai problem.

124. **pray** /pre/ 𐐹𐑉𐐩 —

ᛏᚻ.ᚱᛘ.ᚒᚾᚷ.ᚦᛈ.ᚑᛟ.ᛐᚱ
/ɪn.ʌŋ.wɒv.aʃ.to.tʌ/, HD p. 711
unangwvas|ta

125. **pull out** /pʊl-aᵂt/ ᛐᚸᛚ-ᚦᛐ
— ᚛ᚻ.ᚦᚱ.ᚲᛟ /ɒŋ.kʌ.tʃo/, HD pp.
24, 817 *angqw* 'from, from
there, from or out of that
position, origin or vantage
point' + *tsòopa* 'pull out, extract'

126. **puke** /pʲuk/ ᛐᚹᚦ — ᚻᚴ.ᛝᚵ
/naʲ.jæ/, HD p. 285 *naayö'|a* (v.)
'vomit'; *naayö'i* (n.) 'vomit'

ᚱ. — b.

127. **brother** /brʌðr/ ᚱᛏᚱᛉᛏ —
ᛐᚱᛐ.ᛟᛟ /tʌp.ko/, HD p. 672
tupko('at) 'younger brother'

128. **bread** /brɛd/ ᚱᛏᚴᚨ —
ᛐᚴᛟ /pik/, HD p. 409 *piiki*; MK
p. 203 *piiki*; It is fairly unusual
for the final vowel to be missed
by Shelton. Curiously, the word
also shows up frequently in
Haskell's journal as /pik/,
which he later copied into
English orthography as "peek."
Jacob Hamblin records eating
"peke" on the first mission of
1858,[6] and Gibbons[7] writes of
an Orayvi chief collecting a bag
of "peak" for their return.
Perhaps both Shelton and

Haskell mislearned the word
from the earlier missionaries.

129. **beans** /binz/ ᚱᚦᚻᚷ —
ᛟ.ᚵᚦ.ᚷᛟ.ᚦᛐ /mo.ri.vo.ʃi/, HD p.
251 *morivosi* 'beans, dried beans'

130. **boy** /bɔʲ/ ᚱᚦ — ᛐᚦ.ᛟ
/ti.o/, HD p. 598 *tiyo*; MK p.
216 *tiyo*

131. **blanket** /blæŋkɛt/
ᚱᛚ᚛ᚻᚦᛚᚾ — ᛐᚱ.ᛝᛚᛚ.ᚱ /pʌ.sæl.ʌ/,
HD p. 441 *pösaala*

132. **box** /bɒks/ ᚱᛖᛟᛋ —
ᚒᚴ.ᚻᚦᛈ.ᚩ.ᚷᚱ /wʊ.næʃ.i.vʌ/, HD p.
749 *wuna|sivu* 'wooden box'

133. **butterfly** /bʌtr-flaʲ/
ᚱᛏᚴᛏ-ᛈᛚᚴ — ᚵᛟ.ᛟᛟ.ᚻᚱ /ho.ko.nʌ/,
HD p. 96 *hookona* 'monarch
butterfly'

134. **bull-bait** /bʊl-bet/
ᚱᚴᛚ-ᚱᛁᛐ — ᛐᚱ.ᚷᛈᛈ.ᚻᚴ.ᚻᚱ
/pʌ.vaᵂk.jaʲ.jʌ/, HD p. 432
povok|o(~ya) 'play with an
animal,' 'tease'

135. **bridle** /braʲdl/ ᚱᛏᚴᚨᛚ —
ᚦᚷᛐ.ᛟᛟ.ᚱᛁ /ʃip.mo.ʌt/, HD p. 504
sipmoyi; *-'at* third-person
possessive (so "it's/his/horse's
bridle")

136. **brine** /braʲn/ ᚱᛏᚴᚻ —
ᚷ.ᚱᚻ.ᚱ.ᚷᚦ.ᛐᚦ.ᛚᚱ /e.ʌŋ.ʌ.si.pa.lʌ/,
HD p. 361 *öngaspala*

137. **bark** /bɑrk/ 𐐚𐐆𐐻𐐘 —
Ⱳ𐐄.𐐟 /læp.ʊ/, HD p. 198 *làapu*
'shreddy bark'

138. **breech-cloth**
/brɪtʃ-klɒθ/ 𐐚𐐻𐐺𐐺-𐐄Ⱳ𐐛 —
𐐄𐐄.𐐘𐐻𐐮 /pit.kɪn/, HD p. 416
pitkuna

139. **bed** /bɛd/ 𐐚Ɽ𐐚 — Ⱳ𐐄.𐐄
/ɒp.ʌ/, HD p. 6 *àapa* 'bedding'

140. **basket** /bæskɛt/ 𐐚Ɽ𐐢𐐘Ɽ𐐄
— 𐑉𐐄.Ⱳ𐐄. 𐐛𐐻 𐐚𐐘.𐐘Ɽ.𐐛𐐚𐐘.𐐚𐐤
/ho.ɒp. ɔr ʃi.væ.pʃi.vʊ/, HD pp.
88, 510, 512 *ho'apu* 'wicker
backet'; sivap- (*comb.* of *sivàapi*)
'rabbitbrush' + -sivu (*comb.* of
siivu) 'vessel'

141. **bow** /bo/ 𐐚𐐄 — 𐐄𐐄.𐐑
/aʷt.ʌ/, HD p. 42 *awta*; MK p.
215 *awta*

142. **beads** /bidz/ 𐐚𐐚𐐶 —
𐐛𐐘𐐄.Ⱳ𐐶𐐚.𐐻 /tek.wɒb.ɪ/, HD p.
684 *tuukwavi* 'bead necklace'

143. **bean-harvest**
/bin-hɑrvɛst/ 𐐚𐐚𐐄-𐑉𐐚𐐻𐐚𐐶𐐄𐐄 —
𐐄Ɽ𐐄.𐐑𐐄.𐐄.𐐄𐐄Ɽ /mʌm.ʌr.i.tɒʌ/, HD
pp. 259, 261 *mumri|to(~wisa)*
'go to thresh (as beans)';
mumri(~ya) 'thresh beans';
muri|ta 'be threshing beans'

144. **buckskin** /bʌkskɪn/
𐐚Ɽ𐐄𐐢𐐄𐐻𐐮 — 𐐄𐐄.𐐻𐐤.Ⱳɽ /ʃo.ŋ.wʌ/,
HD p. 525 *sowi'yngwa*

145. **beard** /bir/ 𐐚𐐚𐐻 —
𐐢𐐄.𐐄.𐐘Ɽ.𐐄𐐻 /so.i.tʃʌ.mɪ/, HD p.
526 *sowitsmi* 'beard'; The final ɑ
(/d/) of 'beard' is missing in the
English original.

146. **bees** /biz/ 𐐚𐐚𐐶 — 𐐄𐐄.𐐄𐐄
/mo.mo/, HD p. 244 *mom|o*; MK
p. 215 *momo*

147. **bell** /bɛl/ 𐐚𐐄𐐚 —
𐐛𐑉𐐄.𐐄𐐻.𐐄𐐄 /ejo.kɪn.pi/, HD p.
50 *eyokìnpi*

148. **bear grass** /ber græs/
𐐚𐐚𐐻 𐐛𐐄𐐘 — 𐐄𐐄.𐑉𐐄 /mo.ho/, HD
p. 248 *mooho* 'narrow-leafed
yucca'

𐐚 — b

149. **birds** /brdz/ 𐐚𐐻𐐚𐐶 —
𐐄𐐄.𐐄𐐢.𐐄Ⱳɽ, 𐐄𐐻𐐄.𐑉𐐄.𐐄𐐻
/tʌp.os.kwʌ, ʃɪk.jæ.tʃɪ/, HD pp.
577, 501 *taposkwa* 'canyon
wren'; *sikyats'i* 'goldfinch, lesser'

150. **bad cold** /bæd-kold/
𐐚Ɽ𐐚-𐐄𐐄𐐚𐐛 —
𐐄Ⱳⱱ.𐑉𐐄𐐄.𐐑.𐐄𐐄.𐐄𐐻.𐑉𐑉.𐐄𐐑
/kwaʲ.jʌk.ʌ.mo.kɪ.jʲu.tʌ/, HD p.
168 *kwaayaqmokiw|ta* 'have a
cold'

151. **ball** /bɔl/ 𐐚𐐄𐐚 —
𐐄𐐄.𐑉.𐑉𐑉𐐄.𐐶 /kʊ.ʌ.jʌŋ.æ/, HD pp.

474, 802 *qööngö* 'hard ball used in kicking stone races'

152. **buffalo** /bʌfælo/ ɛⴑʔⴑʟO — ꝺO-ꝺ⨍-⨍⨍ /mo-ʃaʲ-rɪ/, HD p. 252 *mosayru*

153. **black** /blæk/ ɛⴑꝺⵔ — ⵔⵏ.⨍ꝺ.ɛⴑ /kʌ.ɪm.bɪ/, HD p. 472 *qömvi*; MK p. 215 *qőmavi*

154. **blue** /blʲu/ ɛⴑʔ — ꝺꝺⵔ.ⴑⴑ /ʃæk.wꝺ/, HD p. 489 *sakwa* 'blue'

155. **big** /bɪg/ ɛ⨍ꝺ — ⨍O8.ꝺꝺ, ⴑꝺꝺO /hos.kaʲ, wiko/, HD pp. 103, 804, 742 *hoskaya* 'large, huge, enormous'; *wuko-* 'large size'

156. **blunt** /blʌnt/ ɛⴑⵔⵏ — C3C.ⵔⵏ.ꝺⵏ /tʃetʃ.kʌ.æt/, HD p. 651 *tsuku('at)* 'point, tip'; Probably a gavagai problem; Shelton might have pointed at a dull knife, trying to get the word for *blunt,* but got the word for *point* or *tip.*

157. **braided** /bredɛd/ ɛ⨍3ꝺⴑꝺ — ⵔO.ⵔ⨍ⵏ.⨍-⨍ꝺ-ⵏⵔ /ko.kɪn.ɪ-jʊ-tʌ/, HD pp. 473, 476 *qöi(k-)*, *qöqön|ta* 'make a circuit around,' 'make a circular pattern,' including when weaving a basket.

158. **broken** /brokn/ ɛ⨍Oꝺⵏ

— ⨍3-ⵏⵔꝺ-ꝺ⨍ /re-pʌm-tɪ/, HD p. 484 *rupàm|ti* 'slip off, come unfastended or apart'; Duplicate of entry 480, but with a slightly different transcription.

159. **bad** /bæd/ ɛⴑꝺ — ꝺꝺ-Cꝺ-ⴑꝺ-ⵏꝺ /ʃi-vi-laʷ-ni/, HD p. 511 *sivi|lawu(~lalwa), sivilawni* 'be paying for misdeeds,' 'being punished,' + *-ni* future tense

160. **believe** /bliv/ ɛⴑꝺC — ⵏⵏ.Cⵏ.ⴑⴑ /tʊp.tʃɪ.wꝺ/, HD p. 672 *tuptsiw|a*

161. **bring** /brɪŋ/ ɛ⨍⨍ⵏ — ⵔⴑ⨍ꝺ.ⵏO /kwɪʃ.to/, HD p. 186 *kwis|to(~wisa)* 'go to fetch, go to get'

162. **boil** /bɔʲl/ ɛⵔⴑ — ⵔⴑC-ⴑꝺ-ⴑꝺ-ⵏⵔ /kwɑ-læ-læ-tʌ/, HD p. 170 *kwalala|ta* 'be boiling'; *kwala(k-)* 'boil, come to a boil, get boiled'; SE p. 159 *kwalalata* 'it is boiling'

ꝺ — t

163. **town** /taʷn/ ꝺꝺ⨍ — ⵔꝺ-ⵏⵏ /ki-æt/, HD p. 137 *kii('at)* 'house, home, building, dwelling place, village'

164. **turkey** /tʌrkɪ/ ⵏⵔ⨍ꝺⵏ — ꝺO.⨍Oⵏ-O /ko.joŋ-o/, HD p. 155

koyongo

165. **twilight** /twa^{j}-la^{j}t/ 𐐻𐐶𐐴-𐑊𐐴𐐻 — 𐑋𐐨-𐑇𐐨𐐹-𐐸𐐮 /mi-ʃip-hɪ/, HD p. 233 *masiphikpu* ‘dusk’

166. **trap** /træp/ 𐐻𐑉𐐰𐐹 — 𐐽𐐲-𐐿𐐪-𐑋𐐲 /tʃʌ-kɑ-mʌ/, HD p. 622 *tsaqam|a(~ya)* ‘set a deadfall’; *tsaqami* ‘deadfall’

167. **tracks** /træks/ 𐐻𐑉𐐰𐐿𐑅 — 𐐿𐐳𐐸.𐐿𐐳.𐐮.𐐻𐐲 /kʊh.kʊ.ɪ.tʌ/, HD p. 161 *kùuku(’at)* ‘prints, tracks,’ *kùuku’yta* make tracks

168. **twins** /twɪnz/ 𐐻𐐶𐐮𐑌𐑆 — 𐑌𐐪.𐐽𐐯𐑂.𐐮.𐐷𐐭.𐐻𐐲 /nɑ.tʃɛv.ɪ.j^{j}u.tʌ/, HD p. 282 *naatsöviwt*

169. **talk** /tɔk/ 𐐻𐐫𐐿 — 𐑊𐐲𐑊.𐐲𐐺-𐐴.𐐷𐐲, 𐐷𐐲𐐰𐐰𐐻𐐲 /lʌl.ʌb-a^{j}.jʌ, jʌæætʌ/, HD pp. 200, 789 *lalvay|a* ‘talk about’; *yu’a’a|ta* ‘speak’; MK p. 231 *lavayti* ‘talk’; *yu’a’ata* ‘talking’

170. **tell** /tɛl/ 𐐻𐐯𐑊 — 𐐪.𐐵𐑌 /ɑ.a^{w}n/, HD p. 4 *aa’awna* ‘tell, inform, relate, notify of’; MK p. 231 *aa’awna*

171. **tarrapin** /tæræpɪn/ 𐐻𐐰𐑉𐐰𐐹𐐮𐑌 — 𐐴.𐐷𐐲 /a^{j}.jʌ/, HD p. 14 *aaya* ‘rattle; traditionally made from gourd, with a wooden handle, now includes rattles made of other materials’; Shedding light on this entry, Haskell writes, “In the evening the Indians painted and rigged themselves out with rattle boxes which consist of gords [*sic*] and turtle shells, the turtle shells they have tied to the right leg just below the knee. These shells have sheeps hoofs [*sic*] so attached to them that every time the person steps in dancing they rattle scandilous. The gor^{a}ds [*sic*] they have in their hands.”[8]

172. **trade** /tred/ 𐐻𐑉𐐩𐐼 — 𐐸𐐳-𐐮-𐐷𐐲 /hʊ-ɪ-jʌ/, HD pp. 118–19 *huya* ‘trade, sell, exchange, barter’; *hùuya* ‘be trading’; MK p. 193 *huùya* ‘sell’

𐐼. — d.

173. **daughter, or son** /dɔtr, ɔr sʌn/ 𐐼𐐫𐐻𐑉, 𐐫𐑉 𐑅𐐲𐑌 — 𐐻𐐨 /ti/, HD p. 591 *ti(’at)* ‘one’s child, daughter, son, offspring’

174. **sheep** /dip/ 𐐼𐐨𐐹 — 𐐿𐐲-𐑌𐐩-𐑊𐐲 /kʌ-ne-lʌ/, HD p. 132 *kaneelo* ‘sheep’; Written 𐐼𐐨𐐹 (/dip/) in the original, and the entire entry is crossed out. The intended word was 𐑇𐐨𐐹 (/ʃip/) ‘sheep.’ Note that the 𐐼 and 𐑇 are near mirror images.

175. **day-break** /de-brek/
ѳ3-ଣ⸲3ѳ — ⋒0᠊⸲⋁ᴎ.୮.ᴨ⸲
/kojæŋ.ʌ.nɪ/, HD p. 480
qöyangwnu 'be white dawn, the
first light of day on the eastern
horizon'

176. **daylight** /de-laʲt/ ѳ3-ᴌ⸲ᴎ
— ᴅ⸲.⋒⸲⋁ᴎ.୮.ᴨ⸲ /ʃɪ.kjæŋ.ʌ.nɪ/,
HD p. 501 *sikyangwnu* 'be
yellow dawn (the second phase
of dawn, when the sky becomes
reddish-yellow just before the
sun rises)'

177. **dusk** /dʌsk/ ѳ୮8⋒ —
ᴨ8-ᴅᴦᴨ-ᴨ୮ /ta-ʃʌp-tʌ/, HD pp.
564, 855 *taasupi* 'twilight, the
yellow-reddish twilight
noticeable along the western
sky after the sun has set'; See
entry 3.

178. **dust, or sand** /dʌst, ɔr
sænd/ ѳ୮8ᴨ, ѳ⸲ 8⋁ᴎѳ — ᴨ3-ⵡᴨ
/te-wɪ/, HD p. 692 *tuuwa* 'sand';
MK p. 229 *tuuwa*

179. **door** /dor/ ѳ⋒⸲ —
⋒ѳ-ѳᴌ-cѳ-ⵡ୮ /ki-vaʲ-tʃi-wʌ/, HD
p. 144 *kivàytsi* (~*va*, ~*miq*,
~*ngaqw*) 'kiva hatchway'; *hitsiva*
'hatchway, entry'

180. **drum** /drʌm/ ѳ⸲୮э —
ᴨ୮.ᴅ⋒⋒.ᴨᴨ.ᴨэ /pʌ.ʃuk.ɪn.pi/, HD

pp. 448, 815 *pusukìnpi*
'percussion instrument'

181. **dark** /dɑrk/ ѳѳᴨ⋒ —
ээ.⸲эѳ /mi.hi/, HD p. 241
mihi(k-) 'become night, get dark'

182. **dancing** /dænsɪŋ/ ѳ⋁ᴨ8ᴨᴎ
— ᴨэ.ᴨ.⸲ᴨ.ѳᴨᴨ.ѳᴨ.ᴨ୮
/tu.ɪ.hɪ.vɪt.kɪ.nʌ/, HD pp. 592,
416 *tiihu* (n.) 'dance'; *pitkuna*
(*comb.* -*vitkuna*) 'kilt'

ɑ. — d.

183. **dress** /drɛs/ ѳᴨ⋁8 —
ɔ୮.c⋁ᴨ.ᴎⵡᴦᴨ.⋒ⱳ3.ѳ୮
/mʌ.tʃæp.ŋwʌnt.kwe.vʌ/, HD
pp. 180, 257, 844
mötsapngònkwewa (*mötsap-*
'cloth'; *kweewa* 'belt, sash')
embroidered ceremonial sash;
The falling tone in
mötsapngònkwewa was noted by
Kenneth C. Hill after the Hopi
Dictionary was published.

184. **dream** /drim/ ѳᴨѳэ —
ᴨᴨэ.ᴑ.⋒୮.ᴨѳ.ѳᴑ.ᴨᴨ
/tɪm.o.kʌ.na.vo.ti/, HD pp. 685,
309 *tuumoki* 'dream'; *navoti*
'teachings, traditions, body of
knowledge, cultural beliefs';
Dream teachings or visions.

185. **dancers** /dænsrz/ ѳ⋁ᴨ8ᴨ6
— ᴑ୮.cѳ.ᴨ୮ /kʌ.tʃi.nʌ/, HD p.

134 *katsin|a*

186. **dry** /draʲ/ ⵄⴼ⵿ —
ⵡⵘ.ⴼ.ⵥⴶ.ⵏⵔ /læk.ɪ.jʊ.tʌ/, HD p.
197 *laakiw|ta* 'be in a dry or
dried state'

187. **drunk** /drʌŋk/ ⵄⴼⵔⵏⵘ —
ⴹⵔ.ⵙ.ⴼⵡ /ʃʌ.o.næ/, HD p. 519
-*sona* 'craver, one who has an
intense liking for'; See entry
481.

188. **dressed** /drɛst/ ⵄⴼⵡⴺⵏ —
ⵥⴷ.ⵥⵔ.ⴼⵔ /je.jʌ.hʌ/, HD p. 795
yuuyaha 'dress, prepare, get
ready for a formal or ceremonial
occasion'; SE p. 56 *yuuyaha* 'he's
putting on ceremonial garb'

189. **disunited** /dɪsjʲunaʲtɛd/
ⵄⴼⵙⵥⵄⴽⴷⵏⴺⵄ —
ⵀ-ⵄ.ⵀⴺⵍ.ⴺⵕ.ⴼⵀ.ⵔⵘ.ⵡⵘ
/n-ɑ.nɛl.ik.ɪn.ʌŋ.wɒ/, HD pp.
274, 275, 277, 708 This entry
remains elusive. Perhaps
something to do with
naanalöq(muy) 'four at a time'
and *unangw|a* 'heart,' or some
form of *naangwu|ta* 'get into an
argument' or *naanahoy* 'apart,
away from each other in
numerous directions.'

190. **drink** /drɪŋk/ ⵄⴼⴼⵏⵘ —
ⵥⴺ-ⵟⵙ /hi-ko/, HD p. 71 *hiiko*
'drink, ingest liquid'; MK p. 193
hiiko

191. **dance** /dæns/ ⵄⴺⴶⵙ —
ⵡⴶ.ⵀⴺ.ⵙⵔ /wʊ.ni.mʌ/, HD p. 750
wunima (sg.) 'be dancing'; MK p.
218 *wunima, tiiva* (pl.)

192. **dodge** /dɒʤ/ ⵄⴺⵥ —
ⵀⵔ.ⵟⵙ.ⵙⵔ /nʌ.kɑ.mʌ/, HD p. 303
naqàm|ta 'evade a quickly
moving object by dodging
behind s.th.'

193. **doctor** /dɒktr/ ⵄⴺⴶⵟⵏ —
ⵏⴶ.ⴼⴺ.ⵟⵡⵘ. /te.hi.kwɒ./, HD pp.
684, 832 *tuuhikya* 'healer,
medicine man'

194. **disbelieve** /dɪsbliv/
ⵄⴼⵙⵖⵍⴺⵖ — ⵏⴶ.ⵖⵔ.ⵡⵔ.ⵀⵔ
/pe.vʌ.wʌ.nʌ/, HD p. 404
peevewna 'doubt'

195. **divide** /dɪvaʲd/ ⵄⴼⴹⴺⵄ —
ⵀⴺ.ⴼⴶ.ⴺ.ⵙⵔ.ⵀⵔ /na.hʊ.i.vʌ.nʌ/, HD
p. 271 *naahuyvani* 'portions,
apportioned thing(s)'

196. **die** /daʲ/ ⵄⴺ — ⵊⵙ.ⵟⴼ
/mo.kɪ/, HD p. 248 *mooki*; MK
p. 218 *mooki*

c — tʃ

197. **child** /tʃaʲld/ ⵟⴺⵍⵄ —
ⵟⴺ.ⵥⴶ /tʃaʲ.jʊ/, HD pp. 625–26
tsay 'young person'

198. **chimney** /tʃɪmnɪ/ 𐐽𐐮𐑋𐑌𐐮 — 𐐿𐐶𐐨𐐽.𐐿𐐮 /kwitʃ.kɪ/, HD p. 186 *kwitski* 'interior chimney hood'; The word *kwitski* refers to the old kind of chimney, with a square hood, as in a traditional *piiki* house. The new kind of chimney is a *pooksi.*

199. **chicken** /tʃɪkn/ 𐐽𐐮𐐿𐑌 — 𐐿𐐬-𐐪𐐿-𐐬 /ko-ɑk-o/, HD p. 154 *kowaako*

200. **charcoal** /tʃɑrkol/ 𐐽𐐪𐑉𐐿𐐬𐑊 — 𐐻𐐩-𐑂𐐲𐑋-𐑅𐐮 /te-vʌm-sɪ/, HD p. 613 *tövumsi*

201. **chief** /tʃif/ 𐐽𐐨𐑁 — 𐑋𐐬𐑍-𐐶𐐨 /moŋ-wi/, HD p. 247 *mongwi* 'leader, head, chief'; MK p. 216 *mongwi*

202. **chop** /tʃɒp/ 𐐽𐐱𐐹 — 𐑇𐐪.𐑂𐐲𐑊-𐐪 /ʃɑ.vʌl-aʷ/, HD p. 488 *saavu|lawu* 'be chopping firewood'; A related word meaning Navajo, *taasavu,* literally means 'head chopper.'

203. **chin** /tʃɪn/ 𐐽𐐮𐑌 — 𐐯.𐐷𐐨.𐐰𐐻 /ɛ.ji.æt/, HD p. 366 *öyi('at)*

𐐖 — ʤ

204. **jar** /ʤɑr/ 𐐖𐐪𐑉 — 𐐽𐐪.𐐿𐐪𐐹.𐐻𐐲 /tʃɑ.kɑp.tʌ/, HD p. 622 *tsaqapta* 'pottery bowl'

205. **ginned cotton** /ʤɪnd-kɒtʌn/ 𐐖𐐮𐑌𐐼-𐐿𐐱𐐻𐐲𐑌 — 𐐻𐐯𐑅.𐐿𐐴.𐑌𐐨 /tɛs.kaʲ.ni/, HD pp. 676, 811 *tusqeni* 'cotton with the seeds picked out'

206. **jump** /ʤʌmp/ 𐐖𐐲𐑋𐐹 — 𐐽𐐬𐐽𐐬 /tʃotʃo/, HD p. 642 *tsotso'|o* (i.) 'be jumping'; MK p. 223 *tso'omti*

𐐗 — k

207. **goat** /kot/ 𐐿𐐬𐐻 — 𐐿𐐰.𐐹𐐨.𐑉𐐲 /kæ.pi.rʌ/, HD p. 133 *kapiira* 'goat'; Error in orig. 𐐿𐐬𐐻 (/kot/) for 𐑀𐐬𐐻 (/got/).

208. **girl** /krl/ 𐐿𐑉𐑊 — 𐑋𐐪.𐑌𐐲 /mɑ.nʌ/, HD p. 218 *maana*; MK p. 221 *maana*; Error in orig. 𐐿𐑉𐑊 (/krl/) for 𐑀𐑉𐑊 (/grl/).

209. **cotton** /kɒtʌn/ 𐐿𐐱𐐻𐐲𐑌 — 𐐹𐐮𐑇.𐐨.𐑂𐐮 /pɪʃ.i.vɪ/, HD p. 442 *pösövi*

210. **canes** /kenz/ 𐐿𐐩𐑌𐑆 — 𐐸𐐬.𐐹𐐪.𐐿𐐪.𐐺𐐮 /ho.pɑ.kɑ.bɪ/, HD pp. 97, 99, 372 *ho-, hoo-* (*comb.* of hoohu) 'arrow'; *hopaqa* 'arrow reed'; *paaqavi* 'reed'

211. **kettle** /kɛtl/ 𐐿𐐯𐐻𐑊 — 𐑇𐐨.𐑂𐐰.𐑇𐐮.𐑂𐐳 /ʃi.væ.ʃɪ.vʊ/, HD p. 511 *siva|sivu* 'metal vessel, kettle, pot'

212. **clothes** /kloðz/ ꘖ—
ꙮ.Ɗ† /jo.ʃɪ/, HD p. 796 *yuwsi*
'clothing, clothes'; MK p. 217
yuwsi

213. **colt** /kolt/ ꙮ—
ꙮ /kʌ.vaʲ.ho.jʌ/, HD p.
136 *kaway|hoya* 'colt';
Diminutive of *kawayo* 'horse.'

ꙮ — k

214. **cottonwood** /kɒtn wʊd/
ꙮ — Ɗꙮ
/ʃʌ.heb.ko.ho/, HD pp. 527, 145
söhöp- (*comb.* of *söhövi*
'cottonwood') + *koho* 'wood'

215. **crack** /kræk/ ꙮ—
ꙮ /kwɒn.ʌk.ʌ.pʊ/,
HD p. 171 *kwánakpu* 'crack,
fracture'

216. **cottonseed** /kɒtnsid/
ꙮ — ꙮ
/pɪtʃ.ɪn.si.vo.sɪ/, HD p. 417
pitsinsivosi

217. **cards** /kardz/ ꙮ—
ꙮ, ꙮ
/ʃe.kʌn.pi, ɔr moʃ.len.jʌ/, HD
pp. 530, 806 *söqànpi* 'card for
cotton or wool'; The second
gloss /moʃ.len.jʌ/ is *mos-* (*comb.*
of *moosa*) 'cat' + *lengi* 'tongue'
= 'cat's tongue.'

218. **canteen** /kæntin/ ꙮ
— ꙮ
/ʃi.væ.wi.ko.rʌ/, HD pp. 498,
736 *siva-* (*comb.* of *siiva*) 'metal'
+ *wikoro* 'water jug'

219. **Colorado** /kɒlredo/
ꙮ — ꙮ
/pi-ʃi.ʃi.vaʲ/, HD p. 415 *Pisisvayu*

220. **cotton harvest**
/kɒtn-harvɛst/ ꙮ—
ꙮ /pɪs.ip.maʷ.tʌ/, HD
pp. 442, 239 *pösöp-* (*comb.* of
pösövi 'cotton') + *maw|ta* 'be
picking'

221. **corncob** /kɒrnkɒb/
ꙮ — ꙮ /ʃe.ʌŋ.ʌ/,
HD p. 529 *sööngö*; MK p. 217
sööngö

222. **cotton blanket**
/kɒtn-blænkɛt/ ꙮ—
ꙮ /o.vʌ/, HD p. 352 *oova*
'wedding robe'

223. **comb** /kom/ ꙮ—
ꙮ /wʊ.ʃɪ/, HD p. 756 *wùusi*
'brush or comb made from
purple hair grass'

224. **corner** /kɒrnr/ ꙮ—
ꙮ /pɪʃ.iv.ɪ.ʌk-ʌ/, HD
p. 442 *pösö* (*pöpsö*, postp.
~*ve(q)*, ~*ngaqw*) 'internal or
interior corner'

225. **cotton cloth** /kɒtnklɒθ/
ⱷⱯⱮⱨⱺⱡⱳⱡ — ꟾⱯ.ꟾⱯⱷ.ⱱ.ⱺⱱ.ꟾⱵⱷ
/tʃæ.tʃæk.ʌ.mɪ.tʃʌk/, HD p. 623
tsatsakwmötsapu 'manufactured
cloth'; See entry 110.

226. **cabbage (wild)** /kæbɛʤ,
(waʲld)/ ⱷⱡⱸⱡⱻ, (ⱳⱠⱡⱸ) — ⱷⱵ.ꟻⱡ
/ɪs.hɛ/, HD p. 126 *ishö* 'a
yellow-flowering mustard plant
(used as food)'; Now hard to
find. It is described as having a
whitish-yellow top with leaves
about 3 inches long. Thorough
washing and steaming is
required to remove the sand and
bitterness.

227. **cracklings** /kræklɪŋz/
ⱷⱵⱡⱷⱺⱡⱵⱮⱸ — ⱳⱸⱺ.ⱱⱷ.ⱺⱵ
/wik.tʊ.kɪ/, HD p. 736 *wiktuki*
'fried fat or suet, cracklings'

228. **caps** /kæps/ ⱷⱡⱵⱸ —
Ⱶⱡ.ⱡⱸ.ⱸⱷ.ⱸⱵ /pæ.la.ʃi.vʌ/, HD pp.
382–83, 370, 498 *pala-* (*comb.*
of *paalàngpu* 'red') + *siiva*
'metal' = 'copper'; Probably
referring to brass percussion
caps used to ignite the
gunpowder in a caplock rifle.

229. **curls** /krlz/ ⱷⱷⱡⱸ —
ⱷⱵ.ⱨⱶⱡ.ꟻⱷ.ⱷⱵ /kʌ.nel.ho.jʌ/, HD
p. 132 *kanel|hoya* 'lamb'; A

kanelhoya /ka'nɛlhoja/ is a lamb
(literally 'sheep + DIM'').
Apparently a gavagai problem;
Shelton pointed at the curly
wool of a lamb, trying to get the
word for curls, and got the word
for lamb.

230. **crow** /kro/ ⱷⱷⱺ —
ⱡⱵ.ⱷ.ⱸⱡ /æŋ.ʊ.ʃæ/, HD pp. 28,
812 *angwusi* 'raven, crow'

231. **corrupt** /kʌrʌpt/ ⱷⱵⱷⱵⱵⱵ
— ꟻⱺ.ⱸⱸ.ⱡⱶ.ⱵⱷⱵ /ho.va.læn.tot/,
HD p. 105 *hovalan|ta* (~*tota*) 'be
wasting'

232. **quick (fast)** /kwɪk,
(fæst)/ ⱷⱳⱵⱷ, (ⱣⱡⱸⱵ) — ꟻⱸⱵ.Ⱶ
/heŋ.ɪ/, HD p. 109 *höngi* 'swift,
fast, fast runner'; SE p. 128
höngyi 'swift in running'

233. **kill** /kɪl/ ⱷⱵⱡ — ⱨⱸ.ⱨⱡ.
ⱷⱵ.Ⱶ.ꟻⱡⱨ.ⱷⱵ /ni.næ. kʌ.ʌ.jæn.tʌ/,
HD pp. 324, 480–81 *niina* (sg.
obj.) 'kill, slaughter, butcher';
qöya (pl. obj.); *qöyan|ta* 'be
killing'; MK p. 224 *niina, qöya*
(pl. obj.)

234. **card (verb)** /kard, (vrb)/
ⱷⱸꟻⱸ, (ⱸꟻⱸ) — ⱵⱵ.ⱷⱵⱨ.ⱵⱵ
/ʃe.kʌn.tʌ/, HD p. 529 *sööqan|ta*
'be carding wool, cotton'

235. **catch** /kɛtʃ/ ⱷⱷⱮ — ⱨⱷ.Ⱶ.

/ŋʊ.ʌ./, HD p. 321 *ngu'a* 'grab, catch'; MK p. 216 *ngu'a*

236. **collect** /kɒlɛkt/ 𐐿𐐱𐑊𐐯𐐿𐐻 — 𐐸𐐬.𐐷𐐬.𐐿𐐲𐑌 /ho.jo.kʌn/, HD p. 107 *hóyokin|ta* 'be moving'

237. **cough** /kɒf/ 𐐿𐐱𐑁 — 𐐩-𐐸𐐩-𐐸𐐩𐐻. /e-he-het./, HD p. 359 *öhöhö|ta* 'be coughing'

238. **cut** /kʌt/ 𐐿𐐲𐐻 — 𐐻𐐳.𐐿𐐮. /tʊ.kɪ./, HD p. 659 *tuku*; MK p. 208 *tuku*

239. **cover** /kʌvr/ 𐐿𐐲𐑂𐑉 — 𐐱𐐿.𐐽𐐬.𐑂𐐲𐑌 /ɒk.tʃo.vʌn/, HD p. 643 This entry remains elusive. Perhaps some form of *tsovala* 'to gather (transitive),' 'assemble 'in a single location.' Gathered crops might have been covered. See entry 259.

240. **cry** /kra^{j}/ 𐐿𐑉𐐴 — 𐐹𐐪.𐐿𐐲.𐑊𐐵𐑌 /pɑ.kʌ.la^{w}n/, HD p. 381 *paklaw|u* 'start to weep, cry'; *paklawna(~ya)* 'make weep, cry'; MK p. 217 *paklawu*

241. **cook** /kʊk/ 𐐿𐐳𐐿 — 𐐿𐐶𐐨-𐑂𐐮 /kwi-vɪ/, HD p. 182 *kwiiva* 'cook by boiling'

242. **cure** /k^{j}ur/ 𐐿𐑏𐑉 — 𐐿𐐱𐑊.𐐲𐐹.𐐻𐐲 /kɒl.ʌp.tʌ/, HD p. 460 *qalaptu* 'get well, recover (from), get cured'

243. **carry** /kærɪ/ 𐐿𐐰𐑉𐐮 — 𐐨.𐑂𐐩𐐽.𐐿𐐲.𐐷𐐳.𐐻𐐲 /i.vetʃ.kʌ.jʊ.tʌ/, HD p. 49 evetskiw|ta 'be sitting astride an animal, be on horseback; SE p. 118 *tsokiwta* 'riding on'; See entry 347.

244. **cross** /krɒs/ 𐐿𐑉𐐱𐑅 — 𐐷.𐐰𐑋.𐐲𐐿𐐲 /j.æm.ʌkʌ/, HD pp. 771–72 *yama(k-)* 'go through, go across, cross'; MK p. 217 *yama*

245. **calf of the leg** /kɑf ɒv ð lɛk/ 𐐿𐐪𐑁 𐐱𐑂 𐑄 𐑊𐐯𐐿 — 𐑇𐐰.𐐸𐐪.𐐰𐐻 /ʃæ.hɑ.æt/, HD p. 488 *saha('at)*; The original manuscript has 𐑊𐐯𐐿 (/lɛk/) for the intended word 𐑊𐐯𐑀 (/lɛg/).

246. **cloud** /kla^{w}d/ 𐐿𐑊𐐵𐐼 — 𐐬.𐑋𐐵 /o.ma^{w}/, HD p. 351 *oomaw*; MK p. 217 *oomaw*

247. **clear** /klir/ 𐐿𐑊𐐨𐑉 — 𐑇.𐐳.𐐰𐑌 /ʃ.ʊ.æn/, HD pp. 808, 599 *suyan* 'easily discernible'

𐐘. — g.

248. **gourd** /gord/ 𐑀𐐬𐑉𐐼 — 𐐿𐑏.𐐮.𐐷𐐰𐐹-𐐮 /k^{j}u.ɪ.jæp-ɪ/, HD p. 164 *kuyapi* 'drinking cup, ladle, dipper'; SE p. 89 *kuyapi* 'dipper for drinking' (made from a gourd)

249. **grass** /græs/ 𐐇𐑄𐑌𐑈 — ᴅꝪ.ᚵᚷ /ʃe.hɛ/, HD p. 527 *söhö* 'galleta grass'

250. **gun** /gʌn/ 𐐇𐑃 — ᚱ.ᛟᚱꝪ.ᚱ.ᚢᚱ /ʌ.mʌk.ʌ.pi/, HD p. 705 *umukìnpi* 'rifle, gun'; MK p. 221 *umukpi*

251. **green** /grin/ 𐐇𐑄𐐼𐑃 — ᛟᛟ.ᛟᚵᚷᚾ.ᛈᛉ /mo.kjɪŋ.pʊ/, HD pp. 243, 822 *mokìngpu* 'bright green emerald color'

252. **glad** /glæd/ 𐐇ᛚᚼᚷ — 𐐇ᛁᛁᚵᚾ.ᛁᛁᚾ.ᚢᛟᚱ /kwɒŋ.wɒ.toʌ/, HD p. 173 *kwángwa'y|ta* 'have a taste for, enjoy'

253. **grind** /graʲnd/ 𐐇𐑄ᛚᚼᚷ — ᚶᛟᛋ-ᚾᛚ-ᚷ /tos-ɪl-aʷ/, HD pp. 606, 604 *tos|lawu* 'be making ground sweet corn,' 'be grinding, crushing'

254. **go** /go/ 𐐇ᛟ — ᚷ-ᚼᚷ, 𐐇ᚵ ᚼᚷ.ᛟᚱ /aʷ-ni, ɔr ni.mʌ/, HD pp. 324, 123, 326 *-ima* (progressive suffix); *nima* 'go home'; MK p. 221 *(-)n(i)* 'go'; *-ma, -wisa* (pl.) 'go along'; *-numa* 'go around'; "Naat nu' awni" [still I go] "I'm still going."

255. **go out** /go aʷt/ 𐐇ᛟ ᚷᚱ — ᚷᚷ.ᛟᚱ /ja.mʌ/, HD p. 771 *yama(k-)* 'come out, emerge, issue'

256. **give** /gɪv/ 𐐇𐑃ᚷ — ᛟᚱꝪ.ᚴ /mʌk.aʲ/, HD p. 230 *maqa*; MK p. 221 *maqa*

257. **growl** /graʷl/ 𐐇𐑄ᚷᛚ — ᚷᛉᛟ /hek/, HD p. 112 *höyku* 'make a loud threatening sound such as a growl or roar'

258. **grin** /grɪn/ 𐐇𐑄𐑄𐑃 — ᚳᚷ.ᚷᚱᛟ.ᛁᚱ /tʃi.jʌm.tʌ/, HD p. 654 *tsuya(k-)* 'become grateful or appreciative, pleased'; See HD, p. 877, section 5.1.1.6, "Many *k*-class verbs replace the -k- with -m- to make a plural stem and add the suffice *-ti.*

259. **gather** /gæðr/ 𐐇ᛚᚷᚵ — ᛚᛟ.ᚳᛟ.𐐇ᚷ.ᚵᚾ /ɒk.tʃo.vaʷ.mn/, HD pp. 34, 643 *aqw* 'to, toward'; *tsovaw|ma* 'go to assemble, gather'; See entry 239.

Ꝫ. — f.

260. **father** /faðr/ ᚵᚷᚷᚵ — ᚼᚷ /na/, HD p. 266 *na('at)*; MK p. 219 *-na*

261. **friend** /frɛnd/ ᚵᚷᛚᚼᚷ — 𐐇ᛁᛁᚷ.ᚳᚵ /kwa.tʃɪ/, HD p. 168 *kwaatsi('at)*; MK p. 220 *kwaatsi*

262. **fire** /faʲr/ ᚵᛚᚷ — ᚶᚷ-ᛇᚶ /te-bʊ/, HD p. 612 *töövu*

'glowing ember, live coal'

263. **fireplace** /faʲrples/
ᕈ𐐼ᕈᒪ𐐲𐑈 — ᗝᒋ.ᒧ.ᗝᒋ.ᒋ
/kʌ.ʌp.kʌ.ʌ/, HD p. 475 *qöpqö*

264. **fathom** /faðm/ ᕈ𐐁ᕟᗝ —
ᗝᒋᗄᒋ.𐐲ᐩ /mʌmp.kɪ/, HD p. 226
màmki 'a length measure of both
outstretched arms (fingertip to
fingertip), fathom (in the Old
English sense)'; Note the
epenthetic /p/ in the
transcription, still heard today.

265. **fawn** /fɔn/ ᕈᗝᕟ —
ᒋᗄ.ᒐᔕ.ᕟᗝ.𐑀ᒋ /pi.æs.ho.jʌ/, HD
pp. 419, 818 *piyar|hoya* 'fawn or
antelope kid'

266. **fox** /fɒks/ ᕈᒐ𐐀𐑈 —
𐐼ᐩ.ᗝ𐑀ᒐ.ᒐᗄ /ʃi.kjæ.taʲ/, HD p. 500
sikyàatayo 'red fox'

267. **full** /fʊl/ ᕈᖁᒪ —
ᗝ.ᒋᗝ.𐐲ᐩ.𐑀ᔕ.ᒋᒋ /o.po.kɪ.jʲu.tʌ/, HD
p. 352 *òopokiw|ta* (sg.) 'be full'

268. **fat** /fæt/ ᕈᒍᒋ — ᒪᕟ.ᕟᕘ
/wi.hʊ/, HD p. 733 *wihu* 'fat,
oil, lard'

269. **few** /fʲu/ ᕈᕀ — 𐑈ᕀᔕ.ᗝ𐑀ᒐᒋ
/sʲus.kjæt/, HD p. 546 *susk|ya*
'one-by-one, singly'

270. **foggy** /fɒgɪ/ ᕈᒐ𐐀ᐩ —
ᒋᒋᗝ.ᐩᔕ.ᐩ.𐑀ᒐ.ᒋᒋ /pʌm.ɪs.ɪ.jʲu.tʌ/,
HD p. 385 *pamös'iw|ta* 'be foggy'

271. **forget** /fɔrgɛt/ ᕈᗝᐩᗝᒐᒧ —
ᗝᕘᗄᒐᗝ.ᗝᐩ /ʃʊ.to.kɪ/, HD p. 556
sùutok|i; MK p. 220 *suùtoki*

272. **fight** /faʲt/ ᕈᒐᒧ — ᕟᒐ-ᒋᗄᒪ𐑀
/naʲ-ʌ.wɒ/, HD p. 285 *naayawi*;
MK p. 219 *naayawva*

273. **find** /faʲnd/ ᕈᒐᕘᗗ — ᒋᕈ-ᒪᒋ
/te-wʌ/, HD p. 697 *tuwa*; MK p.
219 *tuwa*

274. **fall** /fɔl/ ᗗᗝᒪ — ᒋᗝ-ᗝᐩ
/po-ʃɪ/, HD p. 426 *pòosi* 'fall,
drop'; MK p. 219 *poòsi*

275. **face** /fes/ ᕈᗗᕸ — ᒐᗄ-ᒪᗄ.ᒋᒋ
/taʲ-waʲ.tʌ/, HD p. 590
taywa('at) (*anat.*) 'face'

276. **foot** /fʊt/ ᕈᒐᒧ — ᗝᕈ-ᗝᕈ.𐑀ᒐ
/kʊ-kʊ.æt/, HD p. 156 *kuk|u('at)*

277. **finger ring** /fɪŋgr-rɪŋ/
ᕈᐩᒧᗗᕘᐩ-ᕀᐩᒧ — ᒋᒧ.ᗝ.ᕸᐩ /tʌŋ.ɑ.bɪ/,
HD p. 575 *tangavi* 'ring for a
finger'

278. **fiddle** /fɪdl/ ᕈᐩᗝᒪ —
ᒪᕸ.ᒪᕸᒧ.𐑀ᒋ /le.len.jʌ/, HD p. 203
leelena 'flutes, non-percussive
musical instruments';
leelen|a(~ya) 'be playing music';
Haskell writes, "Shelton having
got his fiddle done [i.e., made
or repaired] we spent the
evening in diferent [*sic*] shops
[kivas] playing the fiddle and

singing to the Indians much to their amusement as they had never seen a fiddle before.”[9]

𐑂. — v.

279. **valley** /vælɪ/ 𐑂𐐰𐑊𐐮 — 𐐸𐐰𐐿-𐐬𐑊-𐐲 /hæk-ol-ʌ/, HD p. 56 *hakol|a* ‘depression, dip or basin’

𐑃 — θ

280. **thunder** /θʌndr/ 𐑃𐐲𐑌𐐼𐑉 — 𐐲-𐑋𐐲𐐿-𐐮𐑌-𐐱 /ʌ-mʌk-ɪn-ɒ/, HD p. 705 *umu(k-)* (vi.p.)

281. **thin** /θɪn/ 𐑃𐐮𐑌 — 𐐽𐐰-𐐹𐐩-𐐲𐑍-𐐰𐑊-𐐲 /ʧæ-pe-ʌŋ-æl-ʌ/, HD p. 621 *tsapöngala* ‘thin’ (‘not thick’)

282. **thick** /θɪk/ 𐑃𐐮𐐿 — 𐐹𐐩-𐐲𐑍.𐐰𐑊-𐐲 /pe-ʌŋ.æl-ʌ/, HD p. 440 *pööngala*

283. **think** /θɪŋk/ 𐑃𐐮𐑍𐐿 — 𐐶𐐳-𐐶𐐲𐑌-𐑊𐐵 /wʊ-wʌn-lawʷ/, HD p. 757 *wuuwan|lawu* ‘keep thinking, worrying’

𐑄. — ð.

284. **this** /ðɪs/ 𐑄𐐮𐑅 — 𐐹𐐻 /pt/, HD p. 448 *put* ‘him/her/it/that/that one’

𐑅 — s

285. **sun** /sʌn/ 𐑅𐐲𐑌 — 𐐻𐐪.𐐶𐐲 /tɑ.wʌ/, HD p. 566 *taawa*

286. **sister** /sɪstr/ 𐑅𐐮𐑅𐐻𐑉 — 𐐿𐐳-𐐮.𐐻𐐪𐐺.𐐮𐑌-𐐿𐐴 /kʊ-ɪ.tɑb.ɪn-kaʲ/,

287. **spade** /sped/ 𐑅𐐹𐐩𐐼 — 𐐮𐑌-𐐹𐐨 /ɪn-pi/, HD p. 124 *ìnpi* ‘shovel, spade’

288. **saw (tool)** /sɔ/ 𐑅𐐫 — 𐑅𐐨-𐐩-𐑉𐐲 /si-e-rʌ/, HD p. 515 *siyara* (n.)

289. **sun-flowers** /sʌn-flaʷrz/ 𐑅𐐲𐑌-𐑁𐑊𐐵𐑉𐑆 — 𐐱𐐿.𐐲.𐐶𐐳 /ɒk.ʌ.wʊ/, HD p. 8 *àaqawu* ‘wild sunflower’

290. **sun-up** /sʌn-ʌp/ 𐑅𐐲𐑌-𐐲𐐹 — 𐐻𐐪-𐐶𐐲-𐐷𐐪-𐑋𐐲 /tɑ-wʌ-jɑ-mʌ/, HD p. 852 *taawa yama* ‘the sun came up’

291. **steam** /stim/ 𐑅𐐻𐐨𐑋 — 𐑇𐐩.𐑂𐐨.𐐶𐐱𐑍-𐐶𐐲 /ʃe.vi.wɒŋ-wʌ/, HD p. 530 *söviwangw* ‘steam, vapor’

292. **sack** /sæk/ 𐑅𐐰𐐿 — 𐐻𐐩-𐐿𐐲-𐐹𐐳 /te-kʌ-pʊ/, HD p. 659 *tukpu* ‘sack, bag’

293. **saddle** /sædl/ 𐑅𐐰𐐼𐑊 — 𐐷𐐰𐐻.𐐿𐐮𐑌 /jæt.kɪn/, HD p. 776 *yatkuna* (n. sg.) ‘saddle’

294. **salt** /sɔlt/ 𐑅𐐫𐑊𐐻 — 𐐩-𐐲𐑍.𐐲 /e-ʌŋ.ʌ/, HD p. 362 *öönga*

295. **cedar wood** /sidr-wʊd/ 𐑅𐐨𐐼𐑉-𐐶𐐳𐐼 — 𐐶𐐨.𐐶𐐨.𐐿𐐬.𐐸𐐬 /wi.wi.ko.ho/, HD pp. 733, 145

Perhaps *wihu* (*comb.* wi-, wìi-) 'fat, oil, lard' + *koho* 'piece or log of wood,' i.e., greasewood?

296. **seeds** /sidz/ 𐐑𐐩𐐼𐐯 — 𐐒𐐩.𐐉𐐃.𐐟𐐻 /ʃi.vo.ʃɪ/, HD p. 512 *sivosi* (n. sg.) 'seed'

297. **spindle** /spɪndl/ 𐐝𐐻𐐪𐐲𐐯𐐢 — 𐐓𐐑.𐐌𐐊𐐃.𐐜𐐢 /pa.tʊk.jæ/, HD p. 397 *patukya*

298. **sage brush** /seʤ-brʌʃ/ 𐐝𐐩𐐟-𐐇𐐻𐐫𐐒 — 𐐒𐐒.𐐡𐐌𐐓.𐐃𐐃.𐐙𐐃 /ʃe.wɒp.ko.ho/, HD p. 510 *sivap-* (*comb.* of *sivàapi*) 'rabbit brush' + *koho* 'wood'

299. **stone** /ston/ 𐐝𐐻𐐃𐐻 — 𐐃.𐐡 /o.ʌ/, HD p. 355 *owa* (*o'wa*: *comb.* -*'wa*) 'stone, rock'

300. **snow** /sno/ 𐐝𐐻𐐃 — 𐐝𐐒.𐐒𐐌.𐐊.𐐻 /ne.væ.t.ɪ/, HD p. 345 *nuvati*; MK p. 230 *nuvati*

301. **strap** /stræp/ 𐐝𐐻𐐪𐐊𐐓 — 𐐓𐐃.𐐙𐐡.𐐃𐐻 /to.rʌ.kɪ/, HD p. 605 *tóriki* 'bandolier, or anything worn over the shoulder and across the breast, bandolier-fashion'

302. **smooth** /smuð/ 𐐝𐐃𐐃𐐛 — 𐐒𐐑.𐐃𐐛 /ʃʊ.ma/, HD p. 661 *tuma* 'smooth'; Smooth like a *piiki* stone. Spelling mistake (mirrored letter) in the original

Deseret Alphabet: use of 𐐔 for an intended 𐐓. The unaspirated Hopi /t/ is often heard as /d/ by English speakers.

303. **small** /smɔl/ 𐐝𐐃𐐃𐐢 — 𐐙𐐃.𐐛𐐡 /ho.jʌ/, HD p. 106 -*hoya* (diminutive suffix)

𐐝 — s

304. **stingy** /stɪnʤɪ/ 𐐝𐐻𐐪𐐲𐐝𐐻 — 𐐻𐐲.𐐡𐐊.𐐒𐐇𐐌.𐐡 /ɪn.ʌŋ.wɒb.ʌ/, HD p. 709 *unangwaw* 'stingy one, miser'

305. **sick** /sɪk/ 𐐝𐐻𐐃 — 𐐓𐐒.𐐓𐐒.𐐻 /te.te.ɪ/, HD p. 690 *tuutuy|a* 'be sick'

306. **sorry** /sɒrɪ/ 𐐝𐐪𐐻𐐻 — 𐐝𐐒.𐐃𐐛𐐒𐐒 /na.kjaʲt/, HD p. 271 *naakya'y|ta* 'be withdrawn, standoffish, reserved, unsociable, holding back, introverted, timid, shy'

307. **soft** /sɔft/ 𐐝𐐃𐐑𐐓 — 𐐒𐐒𐐙.𐐓𐐒𐐡.𐐓𐐒 /ʃuh.pɪŋ.pʊ/, HD pp. 542, 848 *suphìngpu*

308. **still** /stɪl/ 𐐝𐐻𐐪𐐢 — 𐐃𐐡.𐐕𐐃𐐒.𐐻 /mʌ.tʃov.ɪ/, This entry remains undeciphered.

309. **spin** /spɪn/ 𐐝𐐻𐐪𐐲 — 𐐓𐐃𐐒.𐐓𐐡 /ton.tʌ/, HD p. 602 *ton|ta* 'be spinning wool or cotton'

310. **sing** /sɪŋ/ ȣłͶ — ꓶꝑ.ꟼł⳽.ꝥ /taᵂ.wɪl.aᵂ/, HD p. 588 *taw|lawu* 'be singing'; MK p. 229 *tawlawu* 'sing'

311. **stink** /stɪŋk/ ȣꝯłͶꝰ — ƒꝥ.ꝧꝰ.ꝧ.ꝯł /ho.væk.ʌ.tɪ/, HD p. 105 *hovaqtu* 'smell, have an odor'

312. **sweep** /swip/ ȣɰꝥꝰ — ꝥꝯꝥ.ꜱꝰꝰ /mʌʃ.pɒt/, HD p. 235 *maspa|to* 'go to throw out or sweep away'; *maspa* 'sweep'; MK p. 230 *maspa*

313. **surround** /sʌraᵂnd/ ȣꝯłꝥ⳽ꝥꝥ — ꝯƒ-ꝰꝰ.ꝯꝯ /ʊh-taʲ.jʌ/, HD p. 716 *ùuta(~ya)* 'close, seal, block an entrance or passageway'

314. **sting** /stɪŋ/ ȣꝯłͶ — ꝥꝯ.ꝯ.ꝯͶ-ɰł /mʊ.ʌ.æŋ-wɪ/, HD pp. 258, 850 *mu'a* 'sting (re insect)'

315. **satisfied** /sætɪsfaʲd/ ȣꝯꝯłȣꝯꝯꝥꝥ — 3.ꝯꝯ.ꝯꝯ /e.jʲu.tʌ/, HD p. 363 *ööyiw|ta* 'be satiated, full'

316. **swallow** /swɒlo/ ȣɰꝯɰꝯꝥ — ꝥɰꝯ /kwʊ/, HD p. 188 *kwu'u(k-)* (v.) 'swallow'

317. **snore** /snor/ ȣꝰꝥꝯł — ꝯꝯ.ꝰꝥꝯꝥ.ꝯꝯ /hɛ.roro.tʌ/, HD p. 68 *heroro|ta* 'be snoring'

318. **sleep** /slip/ ȣꝯꝥꝰ — ꝯꝯ.ꝯꝥ /pʊ.wi/, HD p. 452 *puuwi* (v. sg.) 'sleep'; MK p. 229 *puuwi*

319. **stamp** /stæmp/ ȣꝯꝯꝥꝰ — ꝥꝯł.ꝯꝥ.ꝯ /oŋ.ʌk.n/, HD p. 349 *óngokna(~ya)* 'cause to bump into'

320. **steal (verb)** /stil, (vrb)/ ȣꝯꝥꝯ, (ꝯꝰꝥ) — ꝯꝯ.ꝥꝯ.ꝯ /naᵂ.ki.ʌ/, HD p. 311 *nàwki(~ya)* 'deprive one of possession by snatching, grabbing, or by assuming control of'

321. **stab** /stæb/ ȣꝯꝯꝥ — ꝯꝥ.ꝥɰꝯ.ꝥꝰ.ꝯ /ʃe.kwi.kn.ʌ/, HD p. 529 *söökwikna*

322. **swim** /swɪm/ ȣɰłꝰ — ꝥꝥ.ꝥꝥ.ȣłꝯ.ꝯꝰ /mo.mo.sɪ.jæ/, HD pp. 244–245 *momor|i(~ya)* 'be swimming'; (*momorya* 'the action of swimming'); Note the use of /s/ to transcribe the syllable final /r/.

323. **suit** /sʲut/ ȣꝯꝯ — ꝯꝯ.ꝯꝯ.ꝯꝰ.ꝯꝯ /ʃʊ.ɪn.ɪh.pɛ/, HD p. 531 *sú'àape (sú-'inùu-pe)* 'just right for 3P' [i.e., just right for him/her/it]; 'befit, look good in'

324. **sweat** /swɛt/ ȣɰꝯꝯ — ꝯꝥ.ꝥꝯꝯ.ꝥꝥꝯ /na.væl.ket/,

325. **spill** /spɪl/ ȣꝯłꝯ — ɰꝯ.ƒ3 /wɛ.he/, HD p. 732 *wehe(k-)*;

MK p. 230 *wehe*

326. **step** /stɛp/ 𐐝𐐻𐐯𐑅 — 𐐶𐐴𐐩.𐑊𐐩
/kwi.læ/, HD p. 183 *kwila(k-)*
'take a step'

327. **sneeze** /sniz/ 𐑅𐑌𐐨𐑆 —
ε.ɒ𐐩. /a.ʃi./, HD p. 12 *àasi(k-)*;
MK p. 230 *asi*

328. **straighten** /stretn/
𐑅𐐻𐑉𐐯𐐻𐑌 — 𐐽ε.𐐶𐐲𐑌.𐐻𐐲𐑉
/tʃe.kwʌn.tʌ/, HD p. 629
tsìikwan|ta 'be making straight'

329. **smoke (verb)** /smok,
(vrb)/ 𐑅𐑁𐐬𐐶, (𐑂𐑉𐐺) —
𐐽ɒ.𐐽ɒ𐑌.𐑉.𐑌ə /tʃo.tʃoŋ.ʌ.ni/, HD p.
640 *tsootsong|ni* 'to smoke';
tsootsong|o 'be smoking, inhale,
puff'

ⅅ. — ʃ.

330. **sheep** /ʃip/ 𐐟𐐨𐐹 —
𐐶𐑉.𐑌ɜ𐑊.𐑉 /kʌ.nel.ʌ/, HD p. 132
kaneelo

331. **sheep shears** /ʃip-ʃirz/
𐐟𐐨𐐹-𐐟𐐨𐑉𐑆 — 𐐽ε.𐐽𐐶𐑌.𐑌ə.𐐬𐑉
/tʃa.tʃoŋ.ʃi.vʌ/, HD p. 623
tsàatsangwsiva (syn. of
tsatsàngwpi) 'scissors'

332. **sure** /ʃᶴur/ 𐐟𐐲𐑉 — 𐐑𐐬𐑌.𐐶ə
/ʃon.kɑ/, HD p. 519 *son qa*
'surely'

333. **shiver** /ʃɪvr/ 𐐟𐐮𐑂𐑉 —

𐑅.𐑉ə.𐑉ə.𐐻𐑉 /tɛ.ri.ri.tʌ/, HD p.
673 *tururu|ta* 'be shivering'

334. **shear** /ʃir/ 𐐟𐐨𐑉 —
ε.𐑉𐐮𐑊.𐑌.𐐻𐑉 /a.rɪl.æn.tʌ/, HD p. 8
aarilan|ta 'be sheering, cutting
hair', *aarila* 'shear, give a close
haircut to'

335. **shoot** /ʃut/ 𐐟𐐬𐐻 —
𐑉.𐐬𐑉𐐬.𐑌.𐐨 /ʌ.mʌk.ɪn.ɑ/, HD p.
705 *úmukna* 'shoot (a firearm)'

336. **shut** /ʃʌt/ 𐐟𐑉𐐻 — 𐐶𐐬.𐐻ə
/ʊh.taʲ/, HD p. 716 *ùuta* 'close,
seal, block an entrance or
passageway'

337. **shoulder** /ʃoldr/ 𐐟𐐬𐑊𐐯𐑉
— 𐑌ə-𐐬𐑉𐑌-𐐽ə.𐑌 /ʃi-kjæ-tʃi.æt/,
HD p. 535 *sukyaktsi* 'shoulder';
-'*at* third-person possessive

ʏ. — ɾ.

338. **rabbit** /ræbɪt/ 𐐻𐑉𐐺𐐮𐐻 —
𐑌𐐯-𐑂𐐬 /ta-vo/, HD p. 566 *taavo*
'cottontail'; MK p. 207 *taavo*

339. **writing** /raʲtɪŋ/ 𐐻𐑉𐐮𐐻𐑌 —
𐑌𐐻-𐑌𐐻𐐺-𐐻𐑌 /tɪ-tɪb-ɪn/, HD p. 681
tutuveni 'any written matter'

340. **rabbit stick** /ræbɪt-stɪk/
𐐻𐑉𐐺𐐮𐐻-𐑅𐐻𐐮𐐬 — 𐑌𐐽ε.𐐬𐐬.𐑁𐐬
/petʃ.ko.ho/, HD p. 449
puts|koho 'rabbit stick, a flat
boomerang-like stick used for

hunting; used for throwing and hitting it on the run'

341. **ring** /rɪŋ/ ⱡⱡⱵ — Ꝺꝶ-ꬶⱣⱮ.ꞱꝶⱢ-Ɽ /ʃi-vɒŋ.wʌl-ʌ/, HD pp. 498, 318 *siva-* (*comb.* of *siiva*) 'metal' + *ngöla* 'hoop'

342. **rain** /ren/ ⱡꞫⱨ — ⱴꝋ-ⱴꝋꝺ-Ɽ /jo-jok-ʌ/, HD p. 785 *yooyok|i* 'be raining'; MK p. 212 *yooyoki*

343. **rasp** /ræsp/ ⱡꞨꝵꝴ — ⱡꞫ-ꝺꞀꝶⱨ-ꝴꝺ /re-kwʌn-pi/, HD p. 484 *rukwànpi* 'scraper, a device for rubbing or on which to rub back and forth in a filing or stroking motion'

344. **red** /rɛd/ ⱡꝴꝋ — Ꞁꝵ-ꝶꝵ-ꝺꝴ /pæ-læ-pʊ/, HD p. 370 *paalàngpu*; MK p. 228 *paalangpu*

345. **rough** /rʌf/ ⱡⱤꝐ — ꝵⱨ.ꝵ.ⱡꝵ /æn.æ.hæ/, HD p. 22 *anaha'a* (adj.) 'rough, not smooth'

346. **rich** /rɪtʃ/ ⱡⱡꞬ — ꝺⱴꝋ.ⱡꝺꝋ.ⱡ /kja.hɒk.ɪ/, HD p. 190 *kyaahaki* 'rich person'; MK p. 228 *kyaahaki*

347. **ride** /raʲd/ ⱡꝵꝋ — ꝺ.ꬶꞬ-ꝺⱤ.ⱴꝴ.ꝴⱤ /i.vetʃ-kʌ.jʲu.tʌ/, HD p. 49 *evetskiw|ta(~yungwa)* 'be sitting astride an animal, be on horseback'; See entry 243.

348. **run** /rʌn/ ⱡⱤⱨ — Ꞁꝵⱡ.ⱡ.ꝋⱡ /wɒr.ɪ.kɪ/, HD pp. 728, 844 *wari(k-)* 'race, dash'; MK p. 228 *wari, yuùtu* (pl.)

349. **write** /raʲt/ ⱡꝵꝴ — ꝴⱡ.ꝴꬶ.ⱡⱨ.Ꞁꝸ /tɪ.tɪb.ɪn.laʷ/, HD p. 681 *tutuven|lawu* 'be making many marks'

350. **rasp** /ræsp/ ⱡꞨꝵꝴ — ⱡꝺ.ꝺꞀⱨⱨ.ꝴⱤ /re.kwʌn.tʌ/, HD p. 485 *ruukwan|ta* 'be rubbing back and forth in a filing or stroking motion, abrading, sanding, rasping'

351. **rub out** /rʌb-aʷt/ ⱡⱤꬶ-ꝸꝴ — Ꝺꝴ-Ꞁꝸ-ꞀⱡⱮ-ꝸ /ʃʊ-laʷ-wɪl-aʷ/, HD p. 535 *súlaw|lawu(~lalwa)* 'be making disappear, keep erasing, keep diminishing'

352. **reel** /ril/ ⱡꝵꞀ — ⱨꝸ-Ꞁꝵⱡ-Ⱡ /ŋaʷ-wit-ʌ/, HD p. 318 *ngawi|ta* 'making into strands, skeins, be coiling'

353. **rattle** /rætl/ ⱡꝵꞀ — Ꞁꝵ-ⱴꝵ.ⱴꝵ.ⱡⱤ /waʲ-jaʲ.jæ.tʌ/, HD p. 731 *wayaya|ta* 'be loose, capable of moving back and forth, shaking, rocking'

354. **rest** /rɛst/ ⱡꞨꝴꝴ — ꝴꝺ.Ꝺꝺ.Ꞁꝵ.ꝺꝵꞀ-Ⱡⱡ.ꝴⱤ /te.ʃi.wɒ.kɒl-ʌp.tʌ/, HD p. 460

The second part is probably *qalap|tu* 'get well, recover,' but the first part remains undeciphered.

355. **rejoice** /riʤɔⁱs/ ꜟꝺꝩꝏꝏ — ꝼꝏꝼ.ᴜꞔꞔ.ᴦ /hɑh.lɑʲt.ʌ/, HD p. 53 *hàalay|ti* 'become happy, glad'

356. **return** /ritʌrn/ ꜟꝏꝩꞔꝥꝥ — ꝥꝺ.ꝼꝥ-ꝩᴦ /nɑ.ho-jʌ/, HD pp. 14–15 *ahoy* 'go back'

357. **run (as water)** /rʌn, (æz wɔtr)/ ꜟᴦꝥ, (ꝺꝏ ꞎꝺꝥꝥ) — ꝺꝺ.ꝥꝥ.ᴜᴦ /mʊ.ɪn.lʌ/, HD pp. 260–61, 263, 844 *muuna* 'be flowing, running (of liquid)', *munlalay|i* 'be irrigating' (causing water to flow)

358. **wrist (of the arm)** /rɪst, (ɒv ð ɑrm)/ ꝥꝥꞔꞔ, (ꝺꝺ ꝩ ꝺꝥꝺ) — ꝺꝑꞔꞔ-ꝥꝥꝥ-ꝩᴦ-ꝺꝥ /mɒt-pɪk-jʌ-kɑʲ/, HD pp. 238, 860 *matpi|p(aq) (~kye' (~kyaqe), ~po(q))* 'at the wrist joint'

l. — l.

359. **little boy** /lɪtl-bɔʲ/ ᴜꝥꞔᴜ-ꝏꝥ — ꞔꝺ.ꝺ.ꝼꞎꝺ.ꝩᴦ /ti.o.hwi.jʌ/, HD p. 598 *tiyòoya*; The modern form *tiyòoya* is explained as *tiyo* 'boy' + <-`ya>, a variant of the diminutive <-hoya> used after

/o/.[10] The vocabulary transcription appears to reflect an earlier, pre-falling-tone combination of *tiyo* + *-hwija* or a misheard *-hoja*. See entry 360.

360. **little girl** /lɪtl-grl/ ᴜꝥꞔᴜ-ꝏꝥᴜ — ꞔꝺ.ꝥꝺ.ꝼꞎꝺ.ꝩᴦ /mɑ.nɑ.hwi.jʌ/, HD p. 227 *manàwya*; The modern form *manàwya* is explained as *maana* 'girl' + <-`wya>, a variant of the diminutive <-hoya> used after vowels other than /o/.[11] The vocabulary transcription appears to reflect an earlier, pre-falling-tone combination of *maana* + *-hwija* or a misheard *-hoja*. See entry 359.

361. **looking-glass** /lʊkɪŋ-glæs/ ᴜꞔꝺꞔꞔ-ꝏᴜꝺꝥ — ꞔꝺꝥ.ꞔꞔ.Cᴦ /pæn.ʌp.ʧʌ/, HD p. 386 *panaptsa*

362. **lamb** /læm/ ᴜꝺꝺ — ꝺᴦ.ꝥꝥᴜ.ꝼꝺ.ꝩᴦ /kʌ.nel.ho.jʌ/, HD p. 132 *kanel|hoya*

363. **ladder** /lædr/ ᴜꝺꝥꝥ — ꝺꝺꝺ.ᴦ /ʃæk.ʌ/, HD p. 488 *saaqa*; MK p. 224 *saaqa*

364. **leather** /lɛðr/ ᴜꝺꝥꝥ — ꝺꝺ.ᴜꝺꝺ.ᴦ /ko.læʃ.ʌ/, HD p. 147 *kolaasa* 'leather, leather strap'

365. **lightning** /laʲtnɪŋ/ ᴌɹᑎᚻᛏᴎ
— ᑎᴦᴧᵣᴌᎧᴎᎧᎧᴴ
/tæl.ʌ.wi.pi-k.n/, HD p. 572
talwìipiki (n. sg.); *talwìipi(k-)* 'for
lightning to flash'

366. **louse** /laʷs/ ᴌᎧᎧ — Ꭷᴎᵣᴦ
/ɑt.ʌ/, HD pp. 39, 831 *at|u*
'head louse'; Haskell wrote,
"Come home, stript off, and put
in my time awhile in the highly
respectable and exciting sport of
louse hunting—succeeded in
capturing several. We find it
impossible to keep clear of
them."[12]

367. **lead** /lɛd/ ᴌᴊᎧ — ᴼᎧᴴᴎ
/ho.ɪt/, HD p. 806 *ho'at* 'bullet'

368. **laughter** /laftr/ ᴌᎧᴘᎧᴴ —
ᴄᴦᵣᴄᴈᵣᴴᴎᵤᴌᴎ /ʧʌ.ʧe.ɪŋ.wɒ/, HD
pp. 829, 792 *tsutsuy|a* 'laugh';
~yungwa durative suffix

369. **liberal** /lɪbrl/ ᴌᴴᎧᴴᴌ —
ᎧᴌᎧᵣᎧᴌᎧ /kwa.kwɑ/, HD p. 169
Possibly *kwakwhá* 'thank you'
(male speaker), *kwakwha|ta*
'express thanks'; *kuwa'iwta* 'be
generous'

370. **lazy** /lezɪ/ ᴌᴈᎧᴴ — ᴴᴊᵣᴈᵣᴴᴎ
/naʲ.e.næ/, HD pp. 267, 829
ná'öna 'lazy'; MK p. 224 *na'öna*
'lazy one'

371. **little** /lɪtl/ ᴌᴴᴎᴌ —
ᴼᎧ-ᴅᴊᵣᴴᴦ /hi-ʃaʲ.jʌ/, HD p. 74
hìisa|y 'of smaller or indefinite
size, quantity'

372. **low** /lo/ ᴌᎧ — ᴼᎧᵣᴅᴦᵣᴄᴈᵣᴼᴈ
/hi.ʃʌ.vu.he/, HD p. 74 *hìisava*
'short'

373. **love** /lʌv/ ᴌᴦᴈ —
ᴅᴈᵣᴼᴴᵣᵛᴼᴎᴌᴎ /ʃu.hi.joŋ.wɒ/, HD
pp. 557–58 *sùuyongwa(~ya)*
'like, admire or be impressed
with right away'; SE p. 44
suhyongwa 'admiring it,
appealing to him, attracting
him, fascinating him'

374. **laugh** /laf/ ᴌᎧᴘ — ᴴᴈᴴᵣᴦ
/nan.ʌ/, HD p. 277 *naani*
'chuckle, giggle'; MK p. 198
naani 'laugh'

375. **lift** /lɪft/ ᴌᴴᴘᴎ — ᴄᴴᵣᴊᴎᵣᴦ
/ʧɪ.pæt.ʌ/, HD p. 646 *tsöpàa|ta*
'lift, hoist, pick up'

376. **lie** /laʲ/ ᴌᴊ — ᴊᵣᴄᴊᴌᵣᴦ
/æ.ʧæl.ʌ/, HD pp. 38, 830
atsalvayi 'lie, deliberate
misstatement or distortion of
fact'

377. **leg** /lɛg/ ᴌᴊᎧ — ᴼᎧᵣᎧᵛᴊᵣᴊᴎ
/ho.kjæ.æt/, HD p. 89 *hokya*;
-'at third-person possessive

Ɔ. — m.

378. **man** /mæn/ Ɔᴊʜ — ꒒Ɵ.Ꝺᴦ /tɑ.kʌ/, HD pp. 564, 831 *taaqa* 'married man'; MK pp. 207, 225 *taaqa*

379. **mother** /mʌðr/ ƆᴦꝨɟ — иƟ /ŋɑ/, HD pp. 789, 833 *-ngu* (*comb.* form of *yu('at)* for non-3P forms); MK p. 225 *yu-, -ngu*

380. **meal** /mil/ Ɔ∂ꞟ — иꝯ∂ᴴꜱ /ŋʊmɪn/, HD p. 322 *ngumni* 'flour, finely ground corn or wheat' or *ngumn-* (*comb.* of *nguma*) or (*-*)*nguman* (*comb.* of *nguma* or *ngumni*) '(-)grind: cornmeal-' or '(-)cornmeal-'

381. **maid** /med/ Ɔ3Ɵ — ꝺꝯꝯꝨ3ꞟƟꝯ /ʃʊphelaᵂt/, HD p. 542 *suphelaw|ta* 'be in the original or pristine state'; Apparently a metaphorical usage. The English word could, in the Deseret Alphabet, also be read as 'made,' but see entry 56, which has the gloss 'young man' for what appears to be the same Hopi word.

382. **mask** /mæsk/ Ɔᴊ8Ɵ — ꒒Ɵ6ƟƟ /pivik/, HD p. 696 This entry is still uncertain. Perhaps

a corruption of *tuviku* 'mask, disguise'; a clerk might have mistakenly copied a ꒒ (/t/) as a ꓶ (/p/).

383. **mud** /mʌd/ Ɔᴦθ — ꞔᴦᴦꝺ-ᴦ /tʃʌʌk-ʌ/, HD p. 647 *tsöqa*

384. **mark** /mɑrk/ Ɔ8Ꝩꝺ — ꒒3ꝯ /pet/, HD p. 402 *pe('at)* 'mark, design, decoration'

385. **mattress** /mætræs/ ƆᴊꝨꜱ8 — ꒒Ɵꞁꝯᴦ /taᵂwʊpʌ/, HD p. 586 *tavupu* 'quilt'

386. **musk melon** /mʌsk-mɛln/ Ɔᴦ8Ɵ-Ɔᴊꞟʜ — ƆᴊꞟƆ.ʜ /mɛlo.n/, HD pp. 240, 832 *melooni*

387. **moon** /mun/ ƆꝺꝘʜ — ƆꝯꝨꝨᴊꞟꝨ /mʲuɪjæwʌ/, HD p. 264 *muuyaw*; MK p. 225 *muuyaw*

388. **moonlight** /munlaʲt/ ƆꝺꝘꞟᴊꝯ — ƆꝯꝨᴊꞟꝨ /mʲuɪtælʌ/, HD p. 866 *muytala*

389. **meat** /mit/ Ɔꝯꝯ — ꝺꝺꝺꞁƟ /ʃikwi/, HD p. 499 *sikwi*; MK p. 225 *sikwi*

Ɔ. — m.

390. **mountain-sheep skin** /maᵂntn-ʃip-skɪn/ ƆꝺꜰꝘꜱ-ꝺꝺꝘ-8ꝺᴴʜ — ꞁꝺꝨ.꒒Ɵ.ꞔꝯ.ꞁ3 /wih.pɑ.tʃʊ.we/, HD pp. 733,

397, 824 Possibly *wìi* 'fat' + *patsvu* 'hide of a young animal'

391. **moccasin** /mɒkɪsn/ ꓷꓪꙨ+ꙸꓦ — ꓩ0.Ꮯ+ /to.tʃɪ/, HD p. 604 *tootsi*

392. **molds** /moldz/ Ꙩ0ꙆꙬꙨ — ꟻ0.ꓱꓩꓩ.+ /ho.tʌp.ɪ/, HD pp. 95, 564 *hoo-* (*comb.* of *hoohu* 'arrow'); *tàapu* 'cradle' (holder, i.e., sides of a mold); Bullet molds are mentioned in Haskell's diary. Bullets were apparently associated with arrows, or at least arrow heads. see HD p. 98 *hoota|to(~wisa)* 'go to make an arrow'; HD p. 95 *hoo-* (*comb.* of *hoohu*) 'arrow'

393. **murderer** /mʌrdrr/ ꙨꓩꟻꙠ++ — Ꙩꓩ.ꙆꙨ.ꙆꙠꙨ.ꓦ /kʌ.la.tak.ʌ/, HD pp. 461, 480 *qalèetaqa* 'warrior'

394. **mechanic** /mɪkænɪk/ Ꙩ+Ꙩꓬꙸ+Ꙩ — ꓦꙠ.ꙨꙄꙠ.ꙄꙨ.ꓕ /na.kwi.so.æ/, HD p. 311 *nawiso'a* 'talented one, one skilled or proficient in the creative arts'

395. **mittens** /mɪtnz/ Ꙩ+ꓵꙸꙶ — ꙨꙠ.ᏟꙠ.ꓦꓩꓦ.ꙸꙠ /ma.tʃi.nʌp.na/, HD pp. 238, 302 *mats-* (*comb.* of *maa('at)* 'hand, arm') + *napna*

'shirt'

396. **mellow** /mɛlo/ ꙨꓦꙆ0 — ꙸ0.ꟻ0.ꟻꙨ /no.jo.jʌt/, HD p. 331 *noyoyo|ta* 'be giving in (as fruit when being pressed)'

397. **much** /mʌtʃ/ Ꙩꓨꮯ — Ꙏꙁ.ꟻꓩꙨ.ꓨ /wu.hɒk.ʌ/, HD p. 754 *wuuhaq*

398. **mad** /mæd/ ꙨꓡꙠ — ꟻ0.ꟻꙥ /jo.hi/, This entry remains undeciphered.

399. **meet** /mit/ Ꙩꙩꙸ — ꙸꙁ.ꓷꙁ.ꙎꙨ /na.ʃaʷ.wʌ/, HD p. 280 *nàasawva(~ya)* 'meet going opposite directions'

400. **move** /muv/ Ꙩ0Ꙡ — ꟻ0.ꟻ0Ꙩ.ꓨ /ho.jok.ʌ/, HD p. 106 *hoyo(k-)*, *hòoyokya* 'move, change position'

4. — n.

401. **knife** /naʲf/ ꙸꙥꓚ — ꓩ0.ꟻ0 /po.jo/, HD p. 435 *poyo*; MK p. 224 *poyo*

402. **noon** /nun/ ꙸ0ꙸ — ꓩꙠ.Ꙏꓬ.ꙸꙁ.ꓷꙁ.+ /ta.wʌ.na.ʃæb.ɪ/, HD p. 567 *taawan(a)sa|ve* 'midday, noon'

403. **nail** /nel/ ꙸꙥꙆ — ꓷꙠ.Ꙡꓩ.Ꙩꙶ.+.ꓚꙶ.+ /ʃi.væ.mu.ɪ.æp.ɪ/, HD p. 510 *sivamu'àapi* 'metal

fastener'

404. **night** /naʲt/ 𐑌𐐴𐐻 — 𐑋𐐨.𐐸𐐨 /mi.hi/, HD p. 868 *mihi* 'it became night'

405. **new** /nʲu/ 𐑌𐑏 — 𐑊𐐬.𐑋𐐪 /lo.mɑ/, HD pp. 207, 2078 *loma-* (*comb.* of *lolma*) 'good, pretty, beautiful, nice, fine, fit, aesthetically pleasing'

406. **noisy** /nɔʲzɪ/ 𐑌𐑎𐑆𐐮 — 𐐷𐐲.𐐰.𐐰𐐻.𐐲 /jʌ.æ.æt.ʌ/, HD p. 789 *yu'a'a|ta* 'be speaking, talking (about)'

𐑋 — m

407. **me** /mi/ 𐑋𐐨 — 𐑌𐐨 /ni/, HD p. 346 *nuy* 'me'; *nuy* 'me'

408. **mine** /maʲn/ 𐑋𐐴𐑌 — 𐐨.𐐸𐐨𐑋.𐐲 /i.him.ʌ/, HD p. 121 *ihimu*

409. **my** /maʲ/ 𐑋𐐴 — 𐐨. /i./, HD p. 121 *i-*; MK p. 225 *i-*

410. **you** /jʲu/ 𐐷𐑏 — 𐐯𐑋 /em/, HD p. 704 *um* (sg.); MK p. 210 *um* (sg.)

411. **your** /jʲur/ 𐐷𐑏𐑉 — 𐐳𐐸 /ʊh/, HD p. 703 *u-*, *ùu-*, *uu-*; MK p. 234 *uù-* (sg)

412. **yours** /jʲurz/ 𐐷𐑏𐑉𐑆 — 𐐳.𐐸𐐳𐑋.𐐲 /ʊ.hʊm.ʌ/, HD p. 704 *úhimu* (sg.) 'belonging to you'

413. **him, or her** /hɪm. ɔr hr/ 𐐸𐐮𐑋. 𐐫𐑉 𐐸𐑉 — 𐐹𐐲𐑋 /pʌm/, HD p. 385 *pam* 'he/she'; MK pp. 201, 222 *pam*

414. **we** /wi/ 𐐶𐐨 — 𐐨.𐐻𐐱𐑋 /i.tɒm/, HD p. 128 *itam*; MK p. 233 *itam*

415. **ours** /aʷrz/ 𐐵𐑉𐑆 — 𐐨.𐐻𐐱𐑋.𐐳.𐐮 /i.tɒm.ʊ.ɪ/, HD p. 128 *itàamu*

416. **our** /aʷr/ 𐐵𐑉 — 𐐨.𐐻𐐱 /i.tɒ/, HD p. 127 *ita-*, *itàa-*; MK p. 227 *itaà-*

417. **who** /hu/ 𐐸𐐭 — 𐐸𐐱.𐐿𐐮 /hɒ.kɪ/, HD p. 859 *hak, hakiy* (acc. sg.); MK p. 233 *hak*

418. **whose** /huz/ 𐐸𐐭𐑆 — 𐐸𐐱.𐐿𐐮.𐐸𐐨.𐑋𐐳.𐐮𐐻 /hɒ.kɪ.hi.mʊ.ɪt/, HD pp. 55, 385, 859 *hakiy* 'which person's' + *himu('at)* 'possessions'; The word *hakiy* followed by the possessed noun has the force of 'whose' or 'which person's.'

𐑋𐐮𐑅𐑊𐐯𐑌𐐮𐐲𐑅 — mɪslenɪʌs

419. **his or hers** /hɪz ɔr hrz/ 𐐸𐐮𐑆 𐐫𐑉 𐐸𐑉𐑆 — 𐐹𐐲𐑋.𐐸𐐨.𐑋𐐳.𐐮𐐻 /pʌm.hi.mʊ.ɪt/, HD pp. 385, 78 *pam* 'that'; *himu('at)* 'possessions'; MK p. 192 *himu*

420. **yes** /jɛs/ ⴿⴑⵛ — O.Ⱳⱻ. /o.wi./, HD p. 357 *owí*; MK p. 234 *owí*

421. **no** /no/ ⵀO — Ᵽⱻ.ⴑ. /ka.ɛ./, HD p. 456 *qa'é*; MK p. 226 *qa'é*

422. **here** /hir/ Ᵽⱻⴿ — ⴿ37 /jep/, HD p. 779 *yep(eq)*; MK p. 231 *yev*

423. **there** /ðɛr/ ⵅⴑⴿ — 737 /pep/, HD p. 406 *pep* 'at that place, in there, on there'; MK p. 231 *pev*

424. **entire** /ɛntaʲr/ ⴑⵀⴑⴿ — 7ⵏⱰ /pʌʃ/, MK p. 372 *paas* 'thoroughly, completely'

425. **dead** /dɛd/ ⱻⴑⱻ — ⴑⵀ.ⴓ /æn.aʲ/, This entry remains undeciphered.

426. **all right** /ɔlraʲt/ ⱺⴑⴿⴑ — ⴑⵀ.ⱺⴓ /æn.tʃaʲ/, HD p. 30 *antsa* (*paus*. *antsáa'*, ~*'a*, ~*'áy*) 'truly, verily, really, in fact, actually'

427. **yesterday** /jɛstrde/ ⴿⴑⵛⴿ ⱻ3 — ⵏⱻ.Ᵽⱺ /ta.vok/, HD p. 566 *taavok*; MK pp. 207, 234 *taavok*

428. **now** /naʷ/ ⵀⵛ — 7ⵏ.ⴿ /pʊ.ɪ/, HD p. 444 *pu'* 'at this moment in time'; MK pp. 203, 226 *pu'*

429. **tomorrow** /tʌmɒro/ ⵏⵏⱺⴿⱺ — Ᵽⱻ.ⵑⱺ /ka.vo/, HD p. 458 *qaavo*; MK p. 204 *qaavo'*

430. **past time** /pæst-taʲm/ ⵌⴑⵛⵏⴑⵑ — Ᵽⱻ.Ɒⴑⵏ.O /hi.ʃæt.o/, HD p. 86 *hisat* (*paus*. *hísato*) 'at some time, when, an indefinite time, once'

431. **when** /hwn/ ⱣⱲⵀ — ⱣⵏⱰ.ⴑⵑ /hiʃ.æt/, HD p. 86 *hisat* 'when?'; MK p. 193 *hisat* 'when?'

432. **why** /hwaʲ/ ⱣⱲⴓ — Ᵽⱻ.ⵀOⱺ /hi.nok/, HD p. 83 *hiniqw* '(sometimes written hinoq, hinoqw)'; MK p. 193 *hinoq*

433. **is it not** /ɪz ɪt nɒt/ ⴿ6 ⴿⵑ ⵀⵑ — ⵀO.Oⱻ /no.ka/, HD p. 329 *nooqa'* 'isn't that the truth'

434. **cannot** /kæn-nɒt/ ⱺⴑⵀ-ⵀⵑ — Oⵀⵀ /ʃon/, HD p. 519 *son* 'can't, cannot, could not, not be possible'

435. **can** /kæn/ ⱺⴑⵀ — OOⵀ.Oⱻ /ʃon.ka/, HD p. 519 *son qa* 'necessarily, surely'

436. **come in** /kʌm-ɪn/ ⱺⵏⱺ-ⴿⵀ — 7ⱻO.ⴿ /pak.ɪ/, HD p. 380 *paki* (sg.) 'enter'

437. **sit down** /sɪt-daʷn/ ⵛⴿⵀ-ⱻⱻⵀ — Oⱻ.ⵑⴑ /ka.tɛ/, HD pp.

465, 487 *qatu* 'sit, sit down, be seated'; MK pp. 204, 229 *qatu* 'sit, sit down'

438. **all gone** /ɔl-gɒn/ Ө𐐢-Ө𐐎𐐅 — 𐐛𐐡𐐢-𐐡-𐐎3 /ʃʊl-ʌ-we/, HD p. 535 *sulaw, sulawu (paus.)* 'absent, missing, none there'

439. **if** /ɪf/ 𐐒𐐡 — 𐐛𐐒𐐅 /ʃɪn/, HD p. 495 *sen* 'whether'; MK pp. 205, 233 *sen*

440. **maybe** /me-b/ 𐐝3-𐐟 — 𐐟𐐒𐐅.3 /bɪn.e/,

441. **with** /wɪð/ 𐐎𐐒𐐅 — 𐐡.𐐝𐐡𐐝, 3-𐐅𐐡𐐔 /ʌ.mʌm, e-nʌŋ/, HD p. 18 *(a)mum*; SE p. 17 *enang* 'with'; MK p. 233 *-mum, -kw*; *Enang* is 'with' in the sense of a "hot dog *with* mustard."

442. **yet** /jɛt/ 𐐛𐐑𐐡 — 𐐅𐐡 /næt/, HD p. 281 *naat* 'still, yet'; MK p. 234 *naat(o)*

443. **not yet** /nɒt-jɛt/ 𐐅𐐡-𐐛𐐡 — 𐐅𐐡-𐐟Ө.𐐑 /næt-kɑ.ɛ/, HD pp. 281, 456 *naat* 'still, yet' + *qa'é* 'no'

444. **what kind** /hwɒt-kaʲnd/ 𐐛𐐎𐐡-𐐟𐐝𐐅𐐟 — 𐐛𐐟𐐅.𐐡𐐡𐐝.𐐡 /hin.tʌk.ʌ/, HD p. 84 *hin|taqa* 'what kind'

445. **this kind** /ðɪs-kaʲnd/ 𐐛𐐒𐐝-𐐟𐐝𐐅𐐟 — 𐐡𐐎𐐅.𐐡𐐡𐐝.𐐡

/pɒn.tʌk.ʌ/, HD p. 390 *pan|taqa* 'that kind, that sort'

446. **that kind** /ðæt-kaʲnd/ 𐐛𐐡𐐡-𐐝𐐝𐐅𐐟 — 𐐛𐐝𐐅.𐐡𐐡𐐝.𐐡 /jæn.tʌk.ʌ/, HD p. 775 *yan|taqa* 'one like this, this kind, this sort'

447. **that is it** /ðæt-ɪz-ɪt/ 𐐛𐐡𐐡-𐐟𐐒-𐐡𐐡 — 𐐡𐐡𐐝.𐐛𐐟𐐡.𐐡 /pʌm.hap.ɪ/, HD pp. 385, 59 *pam hapi* 'he's the one'; The original Deseret Alphabet has the typo ɪs for the intended 𐐡𐐅.

448. **what** /hwɒt/ 𐐛𐐎𐐡 — 𐐛𐐝𐐝.𐐡 /him.ʌ/, HD p. 77 *himu*; MK p. 233 *himu*

449. **which** /hwɪtʃ/ 𐐛𐐎𐐡𐐕 — 𐐛𐐝𐐝.𐐡 /hit.ʌ/, HD p. 74 *hìita dem. acc.* of *himu* 'what-ACC'; MK p. 233 *hìita*

450. **no difference** /no-dɪfrɛns/ 𐐟Ө-Ө𐐡𐐛𐐡𐐝𐐟8 — 𐐅𐐡.𐐛𐐝𐐡.𐐡 /næp.hit.ʌ/, HD p. 277 *naaphiita* or *naap hiita* 'no matter which one'

451. **it is a pity** /ɪt-ɪz-e-pɪtɪ/ 𐐡𐐝-𐐡𐐟-3-𐐡𐐡𐐡 — 𐐡𐐡Ө.Ө.𐐛𐐟 /pʌʃ.o.hi/, HD pp. 393, 347 *pas* 'very' + *ohi* 'exclamation of regret, sense of loss: too bad, darn, it's a shame'

452. **directly** /dɪrɛktlɪ/

𐐼𐐮𐑉𐐰𐐿𐐻𐑊𐐮 — 𐐸𐐪.𐐿𐐨 /hɑ.ki/, HD p. 51 *haaki* 'wait, hold on, wait a minute'

453. **always** /ɔl-wez/ 𐐫𐑊-𐐶𐐩𐑆 — 𐑅𐐲.𐐽𐐩𐐹.𐑅𐐮 /sʌ.tʃep.sɪ/, HD p. 549 *sutsep*; MK p. 213 *sutsev*

𐑋𐐮𐑅𐑊𐐩𐑌𐐮𐐲𐑅 — mɪslenɪʌs

454. **nothing** /nʌθɪŋ/ 𐑌𐐲𐑃𐐮𐑍 — 𐐿𐐪.𐐸𐐨𐑌 /kɑ.hin/, HD p. 834 *qa himu*; MK p. 226 *qa himu*

455. **after a while** /æftr-e-hwaʲl/ 𐐰𐑁𐐻𐑉-𐐩-𐐸𐐶𐐴𐑊 — 𐐰.𐑇𐐬𐑌 /æ.ʃon/, HD p. 36 *ason* 'at some indefinite time later, eventually, in due course, by and by'

456. **morning** /mɔrnŋ/ 𐑋𐐫𐑉𐑌𐑍 — 𐐿𐐪.𐑂𐐬𐑍.𐐲.𐑂𐐲𐐿 /kɑ.voŋ.ʌ.vʌk/, HD p. 467 *qavongvaqw* 'the next day'

457. **far** /fɑr/ 𐑁𐐪𐑉 — 𐐷𐐪.𐑂𐐬.𐐮. 𐐸𐐱𐐿.𐐮𐑇.𐐴 /jɑ.vo.ɪ. hɒk.ɪʃ.aʲ/, HD pp. 767, 770, 59 *yaap* 'far away, at a distance'; *yaavo|ti* 'become farther away, become a long way'; *haq* 'far away, remotely'; *haqsay* 'real far away'; MK p. 219 *yaavaq, yaavo*

458. **near** /nir/ 𐑌𐐨𐑉 — 𐐸𐐴.𐐹𐐬 /haʲ.po/, HD p. 66 *hày|p* 'near, close, close to, nearby'; *hàypo* 'to a place close by'

459. **this side** /ðɪs-saʲd/ 𐑄𐐮𐑅-𐑅𐐴𐐼 — 𐐸𐐴-𐐿𐐮 /haʲ-kɪ/, HD p. 66 *hàykye'* 'along an area close by'

460. **the other side** /ð-ʌðr-saʲd/ 𐑄-𐐲𐑄𐑉-𐑅𐐴𐐼 — 𐐷𐑏-𐐿𐐮 /jʲu-kɪ/, HD pp. 793, 847, 323 Perhaps *yupqöy|ve(q)* 'on the far side of, beyond' or a truncated form of *àngùukye'* or related words ending with the postposition *-gnùuke'* 'along the other side of'

461. **how many** /haʷ-mɛnɪ/ 𐐸𐐪-𐑋𐐰𐑌𐐮 — 𐐸𐐨𐑇.𐐲 /hiʃ.ʌ/, HD pp. 72, 831 hì*isa'* 'how much, how many, what quantity'

462. **that many** /ðæt-mɛnɪ/ 𐑄𐐰𐐻-𐑋𐐰𐑌𐐮 — 𐐷𐐰.𐑇𐐲𐐿.𐐮𐑅 /jæ.ʃʌk.ɪs/, HD pp. 767–68 *yàasa'* 'this amount, this much, this many'; *yàasakis* 'this many times, this often'

463. **crooked** /krʊkɛd/ 𐐿𐑉𐐳𐐿𐐰𐐼 — 𐐸𐐬.𐐽𐐨.𐐽𐐨.𐐻𐐲𐑍 /ho.tʃi.tʃi.tʌŋ/, HD p. 104 *hotsitsi|ta(~tota)* 'be zigzagging'; *hotsitsitoyna(~ya)* 'be making it zigzag'; SE p. 76 *hotsitsi*

'crooked'

464. **dumplings** /dʌmplɪŋz/ ɑɾɔ˥LɨЧ6 — ⵕⵣ⁸.ⵕⵣⵣЧЧ-ⵣⵓ-˥ɨ /kwɑ.kwɒŋ-wʌ-tɪ/, HD p. 172 *kwaakwangwa* (under *kwangwa* 2)

465. **meat stew** /mit-stʲu/ ɔƏ˥-8˥ƌ — Чɨ.ſⵕ.ⵕⵣ⁸6.ɨ /nɪ.ʌk.kwiv.ɪ/, HD p. 335 *nöqkwivi* 'hominy and meat stew' (*nöq-* 'meat' + *kwivi* 'boiled dish')

466. **stewed peaches** /stʲud-pitʃɛz/ 8˥ƌƏ-˥ƏⒸɟ6 — 8ɨ-˥ƏL-ⵕⵣ⁸6.ɨ /sɪ-pɑl-kwiv.ɪ/, HD p. 505 *sipàlkwivi*; *sipala* 'peach' + *kwivi* 'boiled dish'

467. **mush** /mʌd/ ɔſƏ — Ϟſ˥.9.8ſⵕ-ɨ /hʌr.ʊ.sʌk-ɪ/, HD p. 116 *hurusuki* 'blue corn flour mush'; Typo in the original Deseret Alphabet: ɔſƏ (mʌd) for ɔſⵕ (mʌʃ). The Ə and ⵕ are near mirror-images of each other.

468. **stewed pumpkin** /stʲud-pʌmpkɪn/ 8˥ƌƏ-˥ſɔ˥ɵɨЧ — ˥ƌ-˥ſЧ-8ſⵕ-ɨ /pɑ-tʌŋ-sʌk-ɪ/, HD pp. 228, 116, 395 *patang-* (*comb.* of *patnga*, or perhaps an irregular *paatàng-*) 'pumpkin' + *-suki* (mush?); See the

mush-*hurusuki* entry. This word has not previously been recorded, but it is entirely credible. Kenneth C. Hill (personal communication) indicates that *-suki* is a bound form of uncertain meaning, and may be a loan phenomenon. He has recorded it in *paatupsuki*, "a dish of beans and hominy or the verb meaning to make this dish," and the related *tsu'tsipvatupsuki* "make bean soup with roasted fresh corn kernels instead of hominy, or bean soup made with roasted fresh corn kernels instead of hominy." He did find the form *paatàngkwivi* "boiled *squash* or pumpkin" with the *-kwivi* suffix; cf. the entries above for meat stew and stewed peaches.

469. **buffalo robe** /bʌfælo-rod/ ƐſꝂⵣLⵕ-ɨⵕƏ — ɨⵣⵕ-ⵣ⁸6-ſ /hæk-wev-ʌ/, HD pp. 65, 180 Perhaps *hay* 'hanging' + *-kwewa* (*comb.* of *kweewa*) 'belt'; The original Deseret Alphabet reads "buffalo road" but is almost certainly a typo for *buffalo robe*. Perhaps a gavagai problem; Shelton may have

witnessed a Buffalo Dance, pointed to a buffalo robe, and got the word for a hanging belt.

470. **pantaloons** /pæntælunz/ 𐐹𐐰𐑌𐐻𐐰𐑊𐐭𐑌𐑆 — 𐐸𐐬.𐑂𐐨.𐑌𐐲𐐹.𐑌𐐪 /ho.vi.nʌp.nɑ/, HD p. 106 *hovi|napna* 'trousers, pants'

471. **shirt** /ʃrt/ 𐑇𐑉𐐻 — 𐑌𐐲𐐹-𐑌𐐪 /nʌp-nɑ/, HD p. 302 *napna*; MK p. 198 *navna*

472. **leggings** /lɛgɪŋz/ 𐑊𐐯𐑀𐐮𐑍𐑆 — 𐐸𐐬-𐐿𐐷𐐰-𐑌𐐲𐐹-𐑌𐐪 /ho-kjæ-nʌp-nɑ/, HD p. 90 *hokya|napna* 'woolen leggings'

473. **porcupine** /pɔrkʲupaʲn/ 𐐹𐐫𐑉𐐿𐑏𐐹𐐴𐑌 — 𐑋𐐳𐑍.𐐷𐐰.𐐶𐐲 /mʊŋ.jæ.wʌ/, HD p. 263 *muungyaw*

474. **lead bloom** /lɛd-blum/ 𐑊𐐯𐐼-𐐺𐑊𐐭𐑋 — 𐐷𐐰𐑊-𐐪.𐐸𐐪 /jæl-ɑ.hɑ/, HD p. 771 *yalaha* 'hematite, specular iron ore, a mineral with sparkles in it, used in face painting'

475. **sleeve** /sliv/ 𐑅𐑊𐐨𐑂 — 𐑋𐐪.𐑋𐐪.𐐶𐐲 /mɑ.maʷ.wʌ/, HD p. 218 *maamawa*

476. **flint** /flɪnt/ 𐑁𐑊𐐮𐑌𐐻 — 𐑇𐐨𐑂.𐐲 /ʃiv.ʌ/, HD p. 498 *siiva* 'metal, silver'; Confusion of the flint with the steel; see the following entry.

477. **fire-steel** /faʲr-stil/ 𐑁𐐴𐑉-𐑅𐐻𐐨𐑊 — 𐐹𐐨.𐑊𐐪 /pi.lɑ/, HD pp. 409, 412 *piila* 'flint, s.th. used to strike a fire'; Confusion of the steel with the flint; see the previous entry.

478. **orphan** /ɒrfæn/ 𐐱𐑉𐑁𐐰𐑌 — 𐑌𐐪.𐑊𐐪.𐑂𐐬 /nɑ.lɑ.vo/, HD p. 289 *nalavu*

479. **onions** /ʌnɪjʌnz/ 𐐲𐑌𐐮𐐷𐐲𐑌𐑆 — 𐑅𐐨.𐐶𐐨 /si.wi/, HD p. 498 *siiwi*; MK p. 205 *siiwi*

480. **broken** /brokn/ 𐐺𐑉𐐬𐐿𐑌 — 𐑉𐐩.𐐹𐐲𐑋.𐐻𐐲 /re.pʌm.tʌ/, HD p. 484 *rupàm|ti* 'slip off, come unfastended or apart'

481. **drunk** /drʌŋk/ 𐐼𐑉𐐲𐑍𐐿 — 𐑇𐐲.𐐬𐑌.𐐪 /ʃʌ.on.ɑ/, HD p. 519 *-sona* 'craver, one who has an intense liking for'; See entry 187.

482. **dressed** /drɛst/ 𐐼𐑉𐐯𐑅𐐻 — 𐐷𐐩.𐐷𐐲.𐐸𐐲 /je.jʌ.hʌ/, HD pp. 795, 815 *yuuyaha* 'clothe oneself (pl. in ceremonial context)'

483. **similar** /sɪmɪlær/ 𐑅𐐮𐑋𐐮𐑊𐐰𐑉 — 𐐰𐑌.𐐻𐐴 /æn.taʲ/, HD p. 30 *(a)nta* 'be like, similar to, the same as'

484. **lazy** /lezɪ/ 𐑊𐐩𐑆𐐮 —

CO.ᕙ⅃ᕧ.ᒣ /t∫o.jæv.ʌ/, HD p. 643
tsoyavu

485. **straight** /stret/ ᕋᑊᖡᖌᑊ —
ᑊᒪᑊ.ᑕᑊᒪᕤᖡ.ᒣ /tæl.mwɛr.ʌ/, HD p.
570 Perhaps *tal|murìngpu*
'smooth, round and elongated';

The English word could also be
strait.

486. **homely** /homlɪ/ ᖡᐤᕤᑊᖡ —
ᕤᑊ.ᐤᑊᕋ /nɪ.kɪs/, HD p. 338 *nukur-*
or *nukus-* 'bad'; *nukus|hoya* 'ugly
or corrupt one', 'homely'

Index of English-Hopi Vocabulary Entries

Notes

Chapter 1. Introduction

1. The Church of Jesus Christ of Latter-day Saints objects to the usage of the term "Mormon Church" and this book avoids it. However, the term *Mormon* is in fact commonly used, even within the church, to denote its members, organizations, and beliefs, as is demonstrated by the Mormon Tabernacle Choir or the title of Bruce R. McConkie's book *Mormon Doctrine*. The acronym *LDS*, for Latter-day Saint, is also commonly used as an adjective, as in LDS Church.

2. Jacob Hamblin, known as the "Apostle to the Indians," led a full and interesting life as a pioneer, Indian missionary, peacemaker, and general trouble-shooter. The principal source for his many biographies (Bailey, *Jacob Hamblin: Buckskin Apostle*; Corbett, *Jacob Hamblin: The Peacemaker*; Peterson, "Jacob Hamblin"; Brooks, *Jacob Hamblin: Mormon Apostle to the Indians*; Wixom, *Hamblin*) is his autobiography, dictated in later life to stenographer James A. Little (*Jacob Hamblin*), which emphasizes the miraculous and the visionary and was originally published as part of a faith-promoting series for Mormon children. These biographies have a tendency to dramatize Hamblin's life, and the one by Brooks even started as a screenplay. A new biography by Todd M. Compton (*A Frontier Life*) is recommended for its wide-reaching research and academic rigor.

   Hamblin's autobiography mistakenly listed Ira Hatch, rather than James Pearce, as one of the 1859 missionaries, and this error has been repeated ever since. Hamblin's mistake was no doubt an innocent lapse of memory because Ira Hatch did participate in several other missions to the Hopi, including those of 1858, 1860, and 1862–63. Thales Haskell was a good friend of Ira Hatch and at the beginning of his journal of the 1859–60 mission he mentions dining with Hatch before the trip; but during the mission he refers several times to James Pearce and never to Ira Hatch. See Brooks, "Journal of Thales H. Haskell," 70.

3. Orayvi has also been spelled as Oraibi, Oribe, Oraybi, and Orayve, along with other variants. For village names and other Hopi words, we use the now de facto standard orthography defined and used in the *Hopi Dictionary—Hopìikwa Lavàytutuveni* (Hill et al.), which is based on the Hopi Third-Mesa dialect. Where appropriate, traditional transcriptions of Hopi words are provided in parentheses.

4. Compton, *A Frontier Life*, 143–49.

5. See Appendix A.1.

6. Ibid.

7. See Gibbons ("Journal"), as well as Little (*Jacob Hamblin*), Peterson ("The Hopis and the Mormons: 1858–1873"), and Compton (*A Frontier Life*), which treats this mission in detail.

8. Hamblin, Letter to Brigham Young, October 9, 1859. In his original Deseret Alphabet account, Thales Haskell wrote that "Tom [Adair] having concluded to go with us but afterward weakened" (Haskell, *Journal*, October 9, 1859). When he later copied the journal into traditional orthography, the line became "Tom having concluded to go with us but afterward for some cause or other did not go" (Brooks, "Journal of Thales H. Haskell," 70).

9. The majority of the Haskell journal is preserved at Brigham Young University (Haskell, *Journal*), and one leaf survives at Cornell University (*A Leaf from the Journal of Thales H. Haskell*).

10. In the nineteenth century, the Deseret Alphabet was called a "phonetic" alphabet. Modern linguists distinguish *phonetic* transcription, which records minute differences in sound, from *phonemic* transcription, which assigns a letter to each *phoneme* (contrastive sound) in a language.

11. Haskell dated his last journal entry March 27, but he failed to notice that 1860 was a leap year, and so all his March dates are misnumbered by one.

12. Snydergaard, "Village of My Red Brother."

13. This incident is described in greater detail in Appendix A.2.

14. Little, *Jacob Hamblin*, 64.

15. See Peterson, "Jacob Hamblin," 32; and James, *Pages from Hopi History*, 88.

16. One of the most surprising modern uses of the Deseret Alphabet is in a 2010 book of poetry, *La piedra ente la ñeve*, by Josep Carles Laínez, in the Asturian language of Spain, with parallel text in Roman orthography and Deseret Alphabet.

17. International Phonetic Association, *Handbook*. See the website of the International Phonetic Association at http://www.langsci.ucl.ac.uk/ipa/.

Chapter 2. Provenance

1. Sampson, *Writing Systems*, 19, 21.

2. Daniels and Bright, *The World's Writing Systems*, 3.

3. See Okrent, *In the Land of Invented Languages*; Rosenfelder, *The Language Construction Kit*; and Adams, *From Elvish to Klingon: Exploring Invented Languages*, for more information.

4. Regents of the Deseret University, "Minutes."

5. See Regents of the Deseret University, *The Deseret First Book* and *The Deseret Second Book*.

6. Regents of the Deseret University, The Book of Mormon (𐐉 𐐁𐑉𐐄 𐐅𐐇 𐐋𐐄𐐲𐑉𐑋).

7. Regents of the Deseret University, The Book of Mormon, Part I. This book is often misadvertised by used-book dealers as "The Book of Nephi," "The First Book of Nephi," or "Selections" from the Book of Mormon. However, the book is clearly labeled (in Deseret Alphabet) on the cover, spine, and title page as "Part I" of the Book of Mormon, and it contains the full text of the books First Nephi, Second Nephi, Jacob, Enos, Jarom, Omni, and The Words of Mormon.

8. The complete manuscript of the Bible in the Deseret Alphabet exists in the LDS Church History Library, but it was never printed.

9. The abandonment of the Deseret Alphabet was announced in *The Juvenile Instructor*, a church publication, in 1875 (Cannon, "Editorial Thoughts"). The *Church News* section of the *Deseret News* of December 20, 1958, announced that an unspecified number of unsold copies of *The Deseret Second Book* and The Book of Mormon, Part I had been found and offered them for sale at fifty cents each.

10. Romanic spelling reforms are based on letters of the Roman alphabet and modifications of those letters.

11. *Phonotypy* was pronounced and phonemically written /foˈnɒtɪpɪ/, with the stress on the second syllable, by Pitman and would be pronounced by General American English speakers today as /foˈnɑtɪpi/ or /fəˈnɑtɪpi/.

12. See Reed, *A Biography of Isaac Pitman*; Pitman, *Sir Isaac Pitman*; Baker, *The Life of Sir Isaac Pitman*; Kelly, "The 1847 Alphabet"; and Beesley, "Typesetting the Deseret Alphabet with LaTeX and METAFONT."

13. In a particular language, a phoneme is the smallest contrastive unit in the phonology (sound system). At the time of the Deseret Alphabet, the phonemic principle was not fully understood, and the term *phoneme* had not yet been adopted. However, the reformers already had the key intuition that some sound distinctions were significant and others were not. In March 1854, in the first printed introduction to the Deseret Alphabet, it was claimed "to represent the sounds heard in the English Language, as extensively as is deemed consistent, without entering too minutely into nice distinctions, which the ear does not readily catch, and whose omission causes no loss" (*The Deseret Alphabet*; Stout, *Journal of Hosea Stout*, March 24, 1854).

14. Young, Letter to George D. Watt, April 16, 1847. See also Watt, *The Mormon Passage of George D. Watt*, 72.

15. Watt, Letter to Willard Richards, February 5, 1848. Watt's letter even includes a diagram showing the layout of type cases for the 1847 alphabet.

16. See Kelly, "The 1847 Alphabet"; and Pitman, The Holy Bible.

17. Regents of the Deseret University, "Minutes."

18. Ngraphs are sequences of two or more letters used by orthographical convention to represent single phonemes.

19. Ibid., November 29, 1853.

20. Regents of the Deseret University, "Minutes," November 29, 1853.

21. See MacCarthy, "The Bernard Shaw Alphabet." See also http://www.shavian.org/

22. For more information on George D. Watt and his role in creating the Deseret Alphabet, see Watt, "English Convert Used Phonography Skills in Development of Original Deseret Alphabet"; Alder, Goodfellow, and Watt, "Creating a New Alphabet for Zion: The Origin of the Deseret Alphabet"; and Watt, *The Mormon Passage of George D. Watt.*

23. This manuscript in the LDS Church History Library is sometimes known as the "Manuscript History of Brigham Young." There are references to it being kept or copied into the Deseret Alphabet in the *Journal History*, December 19, 1859; and May 3 and 17, 1860. The *Journal History*, a day-to-day chronicle of events in the LDS Church, is also in the LDS Church History Library. It was kept, at least in part, by Richard Bently; see *Journal History*, September 28, 1860.

24. The *Journal History* entry for June 6, 1859 records, "Geo. D. Watt came into the Historian's Office at Pres. Young's request and gave the clerks a lesson in the Deseret Alphabet. Pres. Young had his private ledger opened in the Deseret Alphabet." The clerk who kept the ledger was almost certainly T. W. Ellerbeck (Beesley, "The Deseret Alphabet in Unicode"). The writing of the "History of Brigham Young" switched from traditional orthography to the Deseret Alphabet on April 11.

25. International Phonetic Association, *Handbook*, 28, 42–43.

26. The Deseret Alphabet and the Pitman-Ellis 1847 alphabet, which was its major phonemic model, treat the /ʲu/ vowel in words like *mule* as a single phoneme. See Ladefoged (*A Course in Phonetics*, 77) for a recent discussion and defense of this practice. Although in most English accents the vowels in *mate* and *moat* are diphthongized, the Deseret Alphabet follows Pitman in treating them as the simple "long vowels" /e/ and /o/.

27. In a closer phonetic transcription, this word would be [piːk], which matches the long vowel of the native Hopi pronunciation of the word, spelled <piiki> in the orthography of the *Hopi Dictionary—Hopìikwa Lavàytutuveni* (Hill et al.). The collector of the vocabulary, who we argue was Marion Jackson Shelton, had a pretty good ear, and it is curious that he missed the final /i/ vowel. He likely mislearned the word—before he ever arrived in Hopi—from previous missionaries, who recorded the word as *peke* or *peak* in their letters and journals. For example, Gibbons wrote that "one of the Oriba [Orayvi] chiefs took one of our sacks and went around through the village and got it full of peak which was a kind of bread they bake out of corn meal when baked it is as thin as brown paper" (Gibbons, "Journal," December 8, 1858).

28. The Orayvi village is sometimes known today as Old Oraibi, to distinguish it from Kiqötsmovi (Kykotsmovi), which was once known as New Oraibi.

29. Peterson ("The Hopis and the Mormons: 1858–1873") gives an overview of the fifteen early missions.

30. *Journal History*, June 26; November 14 and 21, 1853.

31. There have been many attempts to explain the origins of the Moqui/Moquitch terms, which the Hopi generally consider foreign and offensive (James, *Pages from Hopi History*, xii, 168). The Paiute word is /moːkwi/. James proposes that the Spanish may have borrowed the Zuñi word *amukwi*, which means "dead" (James, *The Hopi Indians*, 49); and Peter Whiteley in a personal communication also cites the Zuñi *amuukwe* (it is spelled differently in various orthographies), pointing out that the Spanish extended their influence over Hopi from Zuñi, and so their "mohoqui" term was much more likely to come from Zuñi than from Paiute. The official U.S. government designation of the tribe was not changed from Moqui to Hopi until 1924 (James, *Pages from Hopi History*, 184).

32. We are indebted to Bill Shelton, who is researching the life of his great-great-grandfather, for much of our information about Marion Jackson Shelton.

33. *Journal History*, July 29, 1847. The Sheltons were part of the Pueblo detachment of the Mormon Battalion. Brigham Young and the main body of the first company had arrived in the Salt Lake Valley on July 24.

34. In Shelton's journal, the fort's name is written faintly in pencil and appears to be Atchison. However, Atchison was apparently a common mispronunciation and spelling (see Hannum, *A Quaker Forty-Niner*, 189). Fort Atkinson, on the Arkansas River and the Santa Fe Trail, which was passed by the Mormon Battalion, is probably what he intended.

35. Shelton, Letter to George A. Smith, Communication No. 3, January 22, 1859.

36. Cleland and Brooks, *The Diaries of John D. Lee*, 1:186.

37. See Brooks, *The Mountain Meadows Massacre*; and Walker, Turley, and Leonard, *Massacre at Mountain Meadows*.

38. LaJean Purcell Carruth (*Transcription of the Diary of Marion Jackson Shelton, 1858–59*) notes that "Jackson's shorthand is rather simply written; he was apparently a rather new phonographer."

39. Shelton, Letter to George A. Smith, October 11, 1858; also in Turley, *Selected Collections*, vol. 1, DVD 32.

40. *Journal History*, October 11 and 28, 1858.

41. Shelton, Letter to Gentlemen, March 7, 1859. The "gentlemen" addressed are probably the regents of the University of Deseret, who were charged with promoting the Deseret Alphabet reform.

42. Shelton, "Diary 1858 March–1859 June," March 9, 1859.

43. Shelton, Letter to Brigham Young, July 1859.

44. The schwa, written /ə/ in IPA, appears in words like *about* (/əbaᵂt/), *alphabet*

(/ælfəbɛt/), *Cuba* (/kʲubə/), etc. In addition to his June 1859 report and a letter from Orayvi cited later, Shelton proposed adding new letters for schwa-like vowels (Shelton, List of Words for Reference in the Deseret Letter Edition of the Book of Mormon). The addition of a schwa may also have been the subject of a meeting that Shelton had with Brigham Young concerning "some improvements in the Deseret Alphabet"; Young dismissed the arguments as "technicalities" and "the result of education," stating that "if the alphabet was taught to children who had not learned any other they would never realize the difference" (*Journal History*, September 7, 1859).

45. See Pitman, "On Phonetic Printing (1843a)," 137–38; and "On Phonetic Printing (1843b)," 158.

46. Kelly, "The 1847 Alphabet," 259–60.

47. *Journal History*, June 18, 1859.

48. Young, Letter to Jacob Hamblin, September 18, 1859.

49. This "first mountain" is now known as the Hurricane Fault.

50. In his 1881 autobiography, Hamblin wrote, "President Young also put in my charge sixty dollars worth of goods, consisting of wool-cards, spades, shovels and other articles which would be of value to the Indians, with instructions to dispense them in the best manner to create a good influence among them" (Little, *Jacob Hamblin*, 54).

51. Hamblin, Letter to Brigham Young, October 9, 1859.

52. Gibbons, "Journal."

53. Hamblin's autobiography says they arrived on November 6 (Little, *Jacob Hamblin*, 64–65), but the arrival on November 10 is clear from Thales H. Haskell's journal and a Shelton letter cited later.

54. Ibid., 65.

55. Brooks, "Journal of Thales H. Haskell," 81.

56. Ibid., 82.

57. Ibid., 91.

58. Ibid., 90.

59. Ibid., 91. Haskell was, by all accounts, an unusually powerful man and large for his day. Bertram Tsavadawa in a personal communication indicated that Konesoke is a corruption of *honsoki*, which does indeed mean "bear claw" and is a name that would no doubt have been granted by someone of the Honngyam (Bear Clan).

60. Albert E. Smith, who as a young man knew his grandfather, Thales Haskell, indicates that the ripping was done with axes and wedges (Smith, "Thales Hastings Haskell," 37).

61. Brooks, "Journal of Thales H. Haskell," 81.

62. Ibid., 92.

63. When originally established in 1850, New Mexico Territory encompassed modern Arizona, where the Hopi villages are located, and modern New Mexico. A separate Arizona Territory was created in 1863. See Wilkinson, *Fire on the Plateau*, 175.

64. Haskell's journal and another letter by Shelton indicate that the missionaries actually arrived on November 10.

65. Shelton, Letter to Brigham Young, November 13, 1859.

66. When Jacob Hamblin first arrived in Orayvi in 1858, he wrote that "the hostess, apparently surmising that I would not know how to partake of the bean soup without a spoon, dexterously thrust her fingers, closed tightly together, in the dish containing it, and, with a very rapid motion carried the soup to her mouth. Then she motioned me to eat. Hunger was pressing, and a hint was sufficient" (Little, *Jacob Hamblin*, 61).

67. Shelton, Letter to George L.[sic] Smith, R. Bentley, R. Campbell, J.J., J.V., and Others, November 13, 1859.

68. Shelton, Letter to George A. Smith, November 13, 1859.

69. This line is inaccurately transcribed in the *Journal History*, November 30, 1859, and Brooks, "Journal of Thales H. Haskell," 97, as the defiant "this was as far as I would go." The original goal of the mission was to go to the "Moquitches," who were on First Mesa, where the missionaries of 1858 had originally been left. Haskell's journal starts with the words, "I started from Pinto Ranch ... to make a trip to the Moquitch Indians." Shelton was a sickly man, and it is likely that illness or exhaustion prompted his request to stop in Orayvi, rather than continuing to the original goal of First Mesa.

70. The *Journal History* transcription renders "Moqich" as "Moquis." The Hopi villages were, and most are still, located on three mesas extending south from the Black Mesa. As shown in Appendix A.1, the Moquitch village was probably Wàlpi, together with Sitsom'ovi, on First Mesa. Moshamineel is a corruption of Musangnuvi (often transcribed as Mishongnovi), which is a village on Second Mesa, while Orayvi was at the time the only village on Third Mesa. So, starting from Orayvi, the westernmost village, Hamblin was taking a tour of the whole Hopi country before heading home.

71. On November 15, Haskell recorded that Hamblin and the four other men "returned from the Moquitches" to Orayvi. "They said that some Indian had stolen brother Crosbys saddle, revolver, and knife, and several other things belonging to the rest of the boys. I have learned that it was a Navajoe that got them" (ibid., 81).

72. The *Journal History* entry for February 18, 1860 records, "In the evening Jacob Hamblin arrived from Washington County. He had just returned from an excursion to the Moquich.... The Moquitches told Bro. Hamblin that since he was there before, some U.S. soldiers had been to visit them and had given them spades and

hoes and other tools and told them that if the 'Mormons' went there again to kill them. They received Bro. Hamblin and his company very kindly, but would not trade for or buy any tools which Bro. Hamblin brought with him to trade to them. They thought Bro. Hamblin ought to give them the tools as the U.S. soldiers did."

73.   The four men started for home on November 16; Hamblin stayed with Shelton and Haskell until November 17. The first goal of the four men, at an estimated distance of forty miles, was probably Blue Canyon on the Moenkopi Wash, where water could reliably be found. See Appendix A.2.

74.   Haskell comments several times on the honesty of the Hopi, attributing several thefts to the Navajos who frequented the Hopi villages. He also reports wryly that the missionaries had to haul out all their gear and trading goods repeatedly for inspection by the curious Orayvis.

75.   Shelton, Letter to George A. Smith, November 16, 1859. An edited form of this letter appears in the *Journal History* for November 30, 1859; and that version, sometimes inaccurate, was reprinted in Brooks, "Journal of Thales H. Haskell," 97.

76.   Brooks, "Journal of Thales H. Haskell," 83. Kuyngwu, a good friend of the missionaries, was the regent or acting village chief of Orayvi at the time. See Appendix B.1 for more information about the Orayvi chiefs.

77.   Ibid., 84.

78.   Ibid., 93.

79.   Cleland and Brooks, *The Diaries of John D. Lee*, 1:245–47.

80.   Shelton is referring here to the Hopi prophecy that an Elder White Brother, Pahaana (Bahana), would return to restore order to their society. Jacob Hamblin and others believed that the Mormons fulfilled that prophecy. See Appendix B.2.

81.   Beaver Creek was the early missionaries' name for the Paria River, and where it empties into the Colorado later became Lee's Ferry. This letter shows that Haskell and Shelton were also scouting potential sites for Mormon settlement.

82.   Having been assigned to stay with the Hopi for a year, but lasting only four months, Shelton and Haskell may have been a bit defensive about their reasons for leaving. In the *Journal History* entry for May 9, 1860, Shelton also cites "difficulty with the Navajoes"; the failure of their trading plan was also a factor. Like Shelton, Haskell records the kindness and generosity of the Orayvis as the missionaries prepared to depart (Brooks, "Journal of Thales H. Haskell," 94).

83.   Shelton, Letter to Brigham Young, April 3, 1860.

84.   Little, *Jacob Hamblin*, 78, 85. After this mission, Hamblin wrote that "Bro. Thales Haskell's residence of 5 months among the Moquis has made him more proficient in expressing his ideas to them, than his experience of 8 or 9 years has enabled him to do to the Piutes [sic]" (Hamblin, Letter to Brigham Young, May 18, 1863).

85.   The *San Juan Record*, November 10, 1920, reported that Haskell spoke Ute, Navajo,

"Moqui" (Hopi), and Spanish. To that list must probably be added Paiute (Smith, "Thales Hastings Haskell," 87).

86. Ibid., 2, 52.
87. Shelton, "Letter to the Editor."
88. Peterson, "Jacob Hamblin," 21.
89. James, *The Hopi Indians*, 77–81.
90. Dozier, *The Pueblo Indians of North America*, 102.
91. James, *Pages from Hopi History*, 85–94.
92. See Peterson, "The Hopis and the Mormons: 1858–1873," 192; Gibbons, "Diary," 17; and Christensen, "Among the Hopis."
93. Bourke, *The Snake-Dance of the Moquis of Arizona*, 79–80, 330.
94. Steele, Letter to George A. Smith, January 8, 1863.
95. Hancock, "Account of the 1862 Mission."
96. *Millennial Star*, vol. 41, no. 9, March 3, 1879, p. 139.
97. *Millennial Star*, vol. 16, no. 27, July 8, 1854, pp. 418–19; *Deseret News*, April 13, 1854.
98. See Huntington, *Vocabulary of the Utah and Sho-sho-ne or Snake Dialects*.
99. Hill, "Biography of George Washington Hill."
100. See Hill, *Vocabulary of the Shoshone Language*.
101. Gebow, *A Vocabulary of the Snake or Shoshone Dialect (1859 version)*.
102. Gebow, *A Vocabulary of the Snake or Shoshone Dialect (1864 version)*.
103. Brooks, *Journal of the Southern Indian Mission*, 1–44, 152.
104. Pratt, Letter to Orson Pratt, January 30, 1854.
105. *Journal History*, June 4, 1859.
106. Bullock, *Glossary and Account Book*.
107. Gibbons, "Journal."
108. Shelton, Letter to Gentlemen, March 7, 1859. Shelton's journal entry for March 9, 1859 includes, "This evening I met with the elders and taught them Spanish and the Deseret Alphabet."
109. The *Journal History* for August 12, 1859, records that "Prest. Brigham Young received a letter written in the Deseret Alphabet from Henry Eyring, President of the Cherokee mission." The entry for March 7, 1860, records that "Pres. Young called in the Historian's Office and had a letter read, written in the Deseret Alphabet by a man of the Creek Indian Nation by the name of Irving. It was a good letter and showed the intention of the man to preach the gospel to his people."
110. Simpson, *Navaho Expedition*, 98–102, 258–61.
111. See Whiteley ("Bartering Pahos," 375–76, 402–3), who tentatively reconstructs the name as Sikyawaytiwa, meaning "yellow walking," with implicit reference to a red/yellow fox, rather than a wolf.

112. Simpson, *Navaho Expedition*, 246–49.
113. Hancock, "Account of the 1862 Mission."
114. See Fowler and Fowler, *Anthropology of the Numa*, 33, 273–74, 278–81; and Whiteley, *Deliberate Acts*, 41. We thank Peter M. Whiteley for drawing our attention to the Simpson and Powell vocabularies.
115. Cleland and Brooks, *The Diaries of John D. Lee*, 2:284.
116. Holmes, "Journal." This vocabulary is being deciphered by Kenneth Beesley and LaJean Purcell Carruth, an expert in nineteenth-century Pitman shorthand.
117. See Amundsen, "Diaries," 47.
118. See Voth, *Hopi Proper Names* and "Hopi-English Vocabulary."
119. Seaman, "English-Hopi & Hopi-English Dictionary."

Chapter 3. Hopi Language

1.   Hill et al., *Hopi Dictionary—Hopìikwa Lavàytutuveni*. The traditional trapezoidal representation of the vowels in a language is a stylized cross section of the mouth, with the lips to the left and each vowel symbol representing the highest part of the tongue when the vowel is pronounced. See Ladefoged and Maddieson (*The Sounds of the World's Languages*) and information available online at http://en.wikipedia.org/wiki/Vowel_diagram.
2.   See Seaman, *Hopi Dictionary*; and Jeanne, "Some Phonological Rules of Hopi."
3.   Seaman, *Hopi Dictionary*, 147.
4.   Hill et al., *Hopi Dictionary—Hopìikwa Lavàytutuveni*, 863.
5.   Jeanne, "Some Phonological Rules of Hopi," 245.
6.   Some speakers do have [v], and this needs further study.
7.   Whorf, "The Hopi Language," 160.
8.   See Whiteley, *Deliberate Acts* and *The Oraibi Split*.
9.   Jeanne, "Aspects of Hopi Grammar," 12.
10. Voth, "Hopi-English Vocabulary."
11. Seaman, "English-Hopi & Hopi-English Dictionary."
12. Whorf, "The Hopi Language," 160.
13. Ladefoged and Maddieson, *The Sounds of the World's Languages*, 137.
14. Kalectaca, *Lessons in Hopi*, 7.
15. Whiting, *You Can Record Hopi*, 595.
16. Ladefoged and Maddieson, *The Sounds of the World's Languages*, 148–49.
17. International Phonetic Association, *Handbook*, viv.
18. Ladefoged and Maddieson, *The Sounds of the World's Languages*, 138, 149, 164.
19. Ibid.
20. International Phonetic Association, *Handbook*, 177.

21. Malotki, *Hopi Animal Tales*, 523. See also Malotki, *Gullible Coyote*, 160; and Malotki and Lomatuway'ma, *Earth Fire*, 143.

22. Sekaquaptewa and Pepper, *Coyote & the Winnowing Birds*, 74–75.

23. Hill et al., *Hopi Dictionary—Hopìikwa Lavàytutuveni*, 863. These square brackets appear in the original text.

24. Ladefoged and Maddieson, *The Sounds of the World's Languages*, 144–45.

25. Tyler, Field audio recordings of Mrs. Monongya and Ruben Dawahoya.

26. The term *rhotic* describes a variety of sounds, sometimes varying significantly in their articulation, that sound like *r*.

27. In standard IPA, the alveolar tap is notated [ɾ].

28. The term apico-domal (where domal here refers to the hard palate) is often used in Australian or Indian-continent linguistics and is generally considered to be synonymous with the term *retroflex*. Kenneth Hale and Lorraine Honie, in "An Introduction to the Sound System of Navajo," 12–13, write that "the [apical-domal] sound [ẓ] is found in Hopi (where it is normally written with the symbol r̲)."

29. Jeanne, "Aspects of Hopi Grammar," 12.

30. Seaman, "English-Hopi & Hopi-English Dictionary."

31. Epp, *Bible History in the Hopi Indian Language.*

32. In a personal communication on June 6, 2011, Peter M. Whiteley indicated that the Wikwlapi kiva "is the same kiva variously called by A. M. Stephen Si-vap, Siva'pchomo, and Sivwap [see Whiteley, *The Oraibi Split*, I:237]. [The root] Sivàap- refers to rabbitbrush, Sivaptsomo is literally 'rabbitbrush hill[/mound].' Wikwlapi was the kiva for Moomots or [Mischa] Titiev's 'Momtcit,' the Warriors' society. Kuyngwu's association with it may thus be confirmed, since he belonged to the same clan-set (VI–Coyote, Fox, Kookop, etc.) which owned that society/ceremony jointly with the Spider clan. The Sivàap name indicates the kiva's association also with Tuuvi's clan-set (Piikyas-Patki-Sivàap); indeeed Titiev's notes at one point describe Tuuvi as Sivàap clan. Given Tuuvi's long-term association with the Mormons, this may hint that Wikwlapi was his kiva already in 1858, and thus perhaps why Haskell was invited into it."

33. See Voth, "Hopi-English Vocabulary" and *Hopi Proper Names*, 83.

34. Seaman, "English-Hopi & Hopi-English Dictionary."

35. Lomavitu and Duerksen, *A Short Bible-Study.*

36. Ekstrom, *God Lavayiyat Aṅ Puhuvasiwni.*

37. The [h] might be described as a coda consonant or a "preaspiration" feature of the following consonant, which is realized phonetically as an aspiration of the preceding vowel; see Manaster-Ramer, "Genesis of Hopi Tones," and Whorf, "The Hopi Language."

38. Hill et al., *Hopi Dictionary—Hopìikwa Lavàytutuveni*, 864.

39. The pronunciation [wuːxti] is also heard in Musangnuvi.
40. In a personal communication, David Shaul indicated that the 'woman' word in First-Mesa dialect is pronounced [wuːʔti], with a glottal stop.
41. Kroeber, "Shoshonean Dialects of California," 72.
42. Manaster-Ramer, "Genesis of Hopi Tones," 157.
43. Hill et al., *Hopi Dictionary—Hopìikwa Lavàytutuveni*, 830.
44. Jeanne, "Some Phonological Rules of Hopi," 261.
45. Ibid. See also Manaster-Ramer, "Genesis of Hopi Tones," 156.
46. Hill et al., *Hopi Dictionary—Hopìikwa Lavàytutuveni*, 867. See sections 2.1.4.12–2.1.4.14 for similar alternation examples. See also entry 179 in the English-Hopi vocabulary, this volume.
47. Voth, "Hopi-English Vocabulary," 1.
48. Seaman, "English-Hopi & Hopi-English Dictionary," 194.

Chapter 4. The 1860 English-Hopi Vocabulary

1. See entries 56, 123, 189, 239, 286, 308, 324, 354, 357, 382, 398, 425, 440, 457, 459, 460, and 485.
2. Quine, *Word and Object*, 29, 40, 51–54.

Appendix A. Hopi Locations

1. Gibbons, "Journal."
2. Brooks, "Journal of Thales H. Haskell," 84.
3. Powell, *The Hopi Villages*, 16.
4. See Beadle, *The Undeveloped West*, 576, 587; and *Western Wilds*, 277.
5. Powell, "Journal," 466.
6. Bullock, *Sketches of Route from Washington City to the Moquitch Indians, 1860 Feb.*
7. Palmer, Letter at Fort Wingate, NM, to R[?]. S. Parker, Commissioner of Indian Affairs in Washington, DC, December 20, 1869.
8. Roberts, *The Pueblo Revolt*.
9. Hamblin, Letter to Brigham Young, November 25, 1860.
10. McConnell, Letter to George A. Smith, December 22, 1860. See also Hamblin's autobiography (Little, *Jacob Hamblin*, chapter 10).
11. Flake, "A History of Mormon Missionary Work," 107–8.
12. *St. Johns Herald-Observer*, March 26, 1938; May 21, 1938.
13. See Steele, Letter to George A. Smith, January 8, 1863; Steele, "Map 1863"; Bleak, "Fragment of Journal"; Christensen, Letter to Anthony Ivins, January 23, 1923; Christensen, Letter to Anthony Ivins, September 30, 1923; and Powell, "Journal," 460.

Appendix B. Hopi People and Legends

1. Haskell, "Diary of Thales H. Haskell."
2. Brooks, "Journal of Thales H. Haskell."
3. Whiteley, *Rethinking Hopi Ethnography*, 70.
4. Titiev, *Old Oraibi*, 72.
5. Whiteley, *Deliberate Acts*, 33.
6. Smart and Smart, *Over the Rim*, 79, 125.
7. Ibid., 122, 227–28.
8. Compton, *A Frontier Life*, 133.
9. Hamblin, Letter to Brigham Young, December 18, 1858.
10. Brooks, "Journal of Thales H. Haskell," 93.
11. See Little, *Jacob Hamblin*, and Peterson, "The Hopis and the Mormons: 1858–1873."
12. Whiteley, *Deliberate Acts*, 270–71, 329n8.
13. See Shelton, Letter to Brigham Young, April 3, 1860; and Shelton, "Letter to the Editor," November 10, 1869.
14. See James, *The Hopi Indians*, 48–49; and Geertz, *The Invention of Prophecy*, 29, 120–21.
15. Geertz, *The Invention of Prophecy*, 69.
16. Ibid., 66–68, 120–21, 137–39, 172, 234, 427.

Format of the 1860 English-Hopi Vocabulary

1. See Kalectaca, *Lessons in Hopi*; Seaman, *Hopi Dictionary*; and Hill et al., *Hopi Dictionary—Hopìikwa Lavàytutuveni*.

Text of the 1860 English-Hopi Vocabulary

1. Brooks, "Journal of Thales H. Haskell," 90.
2. Ibid., 92.
3. Ibid., 91.
4. Ibid., 88.
5. Ibid., 89.
6. Little, *Jacob Hamblin*, 61.
7. Gibbons, "Journal."
8. Brooks, "Journal of Thales H. Haskell," 86.
9. Ibid., 88–89.

10.   Hill et al., *Hopi Dictionary—Hopìikwa Lavàytutuveni*, 106, 830.
11.   Ibid.
12.   Brooks, "Journal of Thales H. Haskell," 85–86.

Bibliography

Abbreviations

CHL   LDS Church History Library
IJAL   *International Journal of American Linguistics*
UHQ   *Utah Historical Quarterly*
USHS   Utah State Historical Society

Adams, Michael. *From Elvish to Klingon: Exploring Invented Languages.* Oxford: Oxford University Press, 2011.

Alder, Douglas D., Paula J. Goodfellow, and Ronald G. Watt. "Creating a New Alphabet for Zion: The Origin of the Deseret Alphabet." *UHQ* 52, no. 3 (1984): 275–86.

Amundsen, Andrew. "Diaries, 1873–1914." MS 1503, microfilm, including original and typescript, CHL, Salt Lake City; typescript, USHS, Salt Lake City.

Bailey, Paul. *Jacob Hamblin: Buckskin Apostle.* Salt Lake City: Bookcraft, 1948.

Baker, Alfred. *The Life of Sir Isaac Pitman: Inventor of Phonography.* New York: Isaac Pitman and Sons, 1908.

Beadle, John Hanson. *The Undeveloped West; or Five Years in the Territories.* Philadelphia: National Publishing Co., 1873.

Beadle, John Hanson. *Western Wilds, and the Men Who Redeem Them*. Cincinnati: Jones Brothers, 1880.

Beesley, Kenneth R. "The Deseret Alphabet in Unicode." In *Proceedings of the 22nd International Unicode Conference*, vol. 2, paper C10. San Jose, CA: Unicode Consortium, September 2002.

————. "Typesetting the Deseret Alphabet with LaTeX and METAFONT." In *TeX, XML, and Digital Typography*, 68–111. Lecture Notes in Computer Science 3130. Berlin: Springer, 2004.

Bleak, James Godson. "Fragment of Journal." Typescript, St. George temple file, USHS, Salt Lake City, 1864.

Bourke, John G. *The Snake-Dance of the Moquis of Arizona: Being a Narrative of a Journey from Santa Fe, New Mexico, to the Villages of the Moqui Indians of Arizona*. Original work published 1884. Tucson: University of Arizona Press, 1984.

Brooks, Juanita. *Jacob Hamblin: Mormon Apostle to the Indians*. Salt Lake City: Howe Brothers, 1980.

————, ed. "Journal of Thales H. Haskell." *UHQ* 12, nos. 1–2 (1944): 69–98.

————, ed. *Journal of the Southern Indian Mission: The Diary of Thomas D. Brown*. Logan: Utah State University Press, 1972.

————. *The Mountain Meadows Massacre*. Norman: University of Oklahoma Press, 1962.

Bullock, Isaac. *Glossary and Account Book*. Special Collections, J. Willard Marriott Library. University of Utah, Salt Lake City, 1854.

Bullock, Thomas. *Sketches of Route from Washington City to the Moquitch Indians, 1860 Feb.* CHL, Salt Lake City, February 21, 1860.

Cannon, George Q., ed. "Editorial Thoughts." *The Juvenile Instructor* 10, no. 20 (October 2, 1875).

Carruth, LaJean Purcell. *Transcription of the Diary of Marion Jackson Shelton, 1858–59.* CHL, Salt Lake City.

Christensen, Christian Lyngaa. "Among the Hopis." *Times-Independent* (Moab, UT), March 9, 1922, 4.

———. Letter to Anthony Ivins, January 23, 1923. USHS, Salt Lake City.

———. Letter to Anthony Ivins, September 30, 1923. USHS, Salt Lake City.

Cleland, Robert Glass, and Juanita Brooks, eds. *A Mormon Chronicle: The Diaries of John D. Lee, 1848–1876.* 2 vols. San Marino, CA: Huntington Library, 1955.

Compton, Todd M. *A Frontier Life: Jacob Hamblin, Indian Missionary and Explorer.* Salt Lake City: University of Utah Press, 2013.

Corbett, Pearson H. *Jacob Hamblin: The Peacemaker.* Salt Lake City: Deseret Book, 1952.

Daniels, Peter T., and William Bright, eds. *The World's Writing Systems.* Oxford: Oxford University Press, 1996.

The Deseret Alphabet. Single-sheet bi-fold brochure, probably printed with wooden type, Vault M288.8, D457. CHL, Salt Lake City, March 24, 1854.

Deseret News. "Deseret Alphabet Readers Become Collectors Items." *Church News* section. December 20, 1958, 5, 14.

Dozier, Edward P. *The Pueblo Indians of North America.* New York: Holt, Rinehart and Winston, 1970.

Ekstrom, Jonathan, ed. *God Lavayiyat Aṅ Puhuvasiwni: The New Testament in Hopi.* New York: American Bible Society, 1972.

Ekstrom, Molly Ann, and Jonathan Ekstrom. *How to Read and Write Hopi.* Oraibi, AZ: Hopi Action Program, 1973.

Epp, J. B. *Bible History in the Hopi Indian Language: Old and New Testament.* Los Angeles: Grant Publishing House, 1916.

Flake, David Kay. "A History of Mormon Missionary Work with the Hopi, Navaho, and Zuni Indians." Master's thesis, Brigham Young University, 1965.

Fowler, Don D., and Catherine S. Fowler, eds. *Anthropology of the Numa: John Wesley Powell's Manuscripts on the Numic Peoples of Western North America, 1868–1880.* Smithsonian Contributions to Anthropology 14. Washington, D.C.: Smithsonian Institution Press, 1971.

Gebow, Joseph A. *A Vocabulary of the Snake or Shoshone Dialect.* Great Salt Lake City, Utah Territory: Office of the *Valley Tan,* 1859.

———. *A Vocabulary of the Snake or Shoshone Dialect.* Rev. and improved 2nd ed. Camp Douglas, Utah Territory: Daily Union Gazette, 1864.

Geertz, Armin W. *The Invention of Prophecy: Continuity and Meaning in Hopi Indian Religion.* Berkeley: University of California Press, 1994.

Gibbons, Andrew Smith. "Diary of Andrew Smith Gibbons." Typescript, CHL, Salt Lake City, 1877.

———. "Journal." CHL, Salt Lake City, 1858.

Hale, Kenneth, and Lorraine Honie. "An Introduction to the Sound System of Navajo Part One: Articulatory Phonetics." MIT unpublished manuscript. Navajo Linguistics Archive Project, Ken Hale Archive, MIT, Boston, n.d. http://www.swarthmore.edu/SocSci/tfernal1/nla/halearch/halearch.htm.

Hamblin, Jacob. Letter to Brigham Young, December 18, 1858. Brigham Young Office Files 1832–1878, reel 36, box 26, fd 10. CHL, Salt Lake City.

———. Letter to Brigham Young, October 9, 1859. Brigham Young Incoming Correspondence, reel 37, box 27, fd 1. CHL, Salt Lake City.

———. Letter to Brigham Young, November 25, 1860. Brigham Young Office Files, reel 38, box 27, fd 14. CHL, Salt Lake City.

———. Letter to Brigham Young, May 18, 1863. Brigham Young Incoming Correspondence, reel 40, box 29, fd 9. CHL, Salt Lake City.

Hancock, Mosiah Lyman. "Account of the 1862 Mission to the Moquis." MS 570, included with the "Autobiography of Levi Ward Hancock," CHL, Salt Lake City, 1896.

Hannum, Anna Paschall, ed. *A Quaker Forty-Niner: The Adventures of Charles Edward Pancoast on the American Frontier.* Philadelphia: University of Pennsylvania Press, 1930.

Haskell, Thales Hastings. *A Leaf from the Journal of Thales H. Haskell.* Accounts and publications about Indians, #9087, fd 5. Division of Rare and Manuscript Collections. Cornell University Library, Ithaca NY, 1859.

———. "Diary of Thales H. Haskell, 1859–60, copied by the Brigham Young University Library, 1943." Typescript, L. Tom Perry Special Collections, Harold B. Lee Library, Brigham Young University, Provo, UT, 1943.

———. *Journal.* L. Tom Perry Special Collections. Harold B. Lee Library, Brigham Young University, Provo, UT, 1860.

Hill, George W. *Vocabulary of the Shoshone Language.* Salt Lake City: *Deseret News* Steam Printing Establishment, 1877.

Hill, Joseph John. "Biography of George Washington Hill." http://freepages.genealogy.rootsweb.ancestry.com/ ~larsenbrown/Histories/georgewashhillbyjjhill.txt.

Hill, Kenneth C., Emory Sekaquaptewa, Mary E. Black, and Ekkehart Malotki. *Hopi Dictionary—Hopìikwa Lavàytutuveni: A Hopi-English Dictionary of the Third Mesa Dialect with an English-Hopi Finder List and a Sketch of Hopi Grammar.* Tucson: University of Arizona Press, 1998.

History of Brigham Young. CHL, Salt Lake City, 1859.

Holmes, Henry. "Journal of Henry Holmes." MS 426, CHL, Salt Lake City, 1873.

Huntington, Dimick B. *Vocabulary of the Utah and Sho-sho-ne or Snake Dialects, with Indian Legends and Traditions. Including a Brief Account of the Life and Death of Wah-ker, the Indian Land Pirate.* Rev. and enlarged 3rd ed. Salt Lake City: Salt Lake Herald, 1872.

International Phonetic Association. *Handbook of the International Phonetic Association: A Guide to the Use of the International Phonetic Alphabet.* Cambridge: Cambridge University Press, 1999.

James, Harry C. *Pages from Hopi History.* Tucson: University of Arizona Press, 1974.

———. *The Hopi Indians: Their History and Their Culture.* Caldwell, ID: Caxton, 1956.

Jeanne, LaVerne Masayesva. "Aspects of Hopi Grammar." PhD diss., MIT, 1978.

———. "Some Phonological Rules of Hopi." *IJAL* 48, no. 3 (1982): 245–70.

Journal History of the Church. A day-to-day chronicle of events in the LDS Church from 1830 to the present. CHL, Salt Lake City.

Kalectaca, Milo. *Lessons in Hopi.* Edited by Ronald W. Langacker. Tucson: University of Arizona Press, 1978.

Kelly, J. "The 1847 Alphabet: An Episode of Phonotypy." In *Towards a History of Phonetics,* edited by R. E. Asher and Eugénie J. A. Henderson, 248–64. Edinburgh: Edinburgh University Press, 1981.

Kroeber, A. L. "Shoshonean Dialects of California." *University of California Publications in American Archaeology and Ethnology* 4, no. 3 (1907): 66–165.

Ladefoged, Peter. *A Course in Phonetics.* 4th ed. Boston: Heinle & Heinle, 2001.

Ladefoged, Peter, and Ian Maddieson. *The Sounds of the World's Languages.* Malden, MA: Blackwell, 1996.

Laínez, Josep Carles. *La piedra ente la ñeve*. A book of poems in the Asturian language of Spain, with parallel text in Roman and Deseret Alphabet orthographies. Uviéu, Spain: Trabe, 2010.

Ledger C. Brigham Young's financial ledger, kept in the Deseret Alphabet. Special Collections, Merrill-Cazier Library, Utah State University, Logan, UT, 1859.

Little, James A., ed. *Jacob Hamblin, A Narrative of His Personal Experience, as a Frontiersman, Missionary to the Indians and Explorer, Disclosing Interpositions of Providence, Severe Privations, Perilous Situations and Remarkable Escapes*. Original work published 1881. Freeport, NY: Books for Libraries Press, 1971.

Lomavitu, Otto, and J. R. Duerksen. *A Short Bible-Study: Questions and Answers*. Translated 1914–1915, revised 1923–24 by Rev. J. B. Frey and others. n.p., 1924.

MacCarthy, P. A. D. "The Bernard Shaw Alphabet." In *Alphabets for English*, edited by Werner Haas, 105–17. Manchester: Manchester University Press, 1969.

Malotki, Ekkehart, ed. *Gullible Coyote/Una'ihu: A Bilingual Collection of Hopi Coyote Stories*. Tucson: University of Arizona Press, 1985.

———, ed. *Hopi Animal Tales*. Lincoln: University of Nebraska Press, 1998.

Malotki, Ekkehart, and Michael Lomatuway'ma. *Earth Fire*. Flagstaff, AZ: Northland Press, 1987.

Manaster-Ramer, Alexis. "Genesis of Hopi Tones." *IJAL* 52, no. 2 (1986): 154–60.

McConkie, Bruce R. *Mormon Doctrine.* 2nd ed. Salt Lake City: Bookcraft, 1966.

McConnell, Jehiel. Letter to George A. Smith, December 22, 1860. MS 1322, box 5, fd 21. CHL, Salt Lake City.

New, Douglas Allen. "History of the Deseret Alphabet and Other Attempts to Reform English Orthography." PhD diss., Utah State University, 1985.

Okrent, Arika. *In the Land of Invented Languages.* New York: Spiegel & Grau, 2009.

Palmer, A. H. Letter at Fort Wingate, NM, to R[?]. S. Parker, Commissioner of Indian Affairs in Washington, DC, December 20, 1869. National Archives.

Peterson, Charles S. "Jacob Hamblin, Apostle to the Lamanites, and the Indian Mission." *Journal of Mormon History* 2 (1975): 21–34.

———. "The Hopis and the Mormons: 1858–1873." *UHQ* 39, no. 2 (Spring 1971): 179–94.

Pitman, Benn. *Sir Isaac Pitman: His Life and Labors.* Cincinnati: C. J. Krehbiel, 1902.

Pitman, Isaac. "On Phonetic Printing." *The Phonotypic Journal* 2, no. 21 (1843): 137–38.

———. "On Phonetic Printing." *The Phonotypic Journal* 2, no. 23 (1843): 158.

———, ed. The Holy Bible. Printed in phonotypy using the 1847 alphabet. London: Fred Pitman, 1850.

Powell, John Wesley. *The Hopi Villages: The Ancient Province of Tusayan.* Reprint of an article from *Scribner's Monthly* 11, no. 2 (December 1875): 193–213. Palmer Lake, CO: Filter Press, 1972.

Powell, W. C. "Journal of W. C. Powell." In *The Exploration of the Colorado River and the High Plateaus of Utah by the Second Powell Expedition of 1871–1872*, edited by Herbert E. Gregory, William Culp Darrah, and Charles Kelly. Salt Lake City, UT: University of Utah Press, 2009.

Pratt, Parley P. Letter to Orson Pratt, January 30, 1854. Orson Pratt Family Collection. CHL, Salt Lake City.

Quine, W. V. O. *Word and Object.* Cambridge, MA: MIT Press, 1960.

Reed, Thomas Allen. *A Biography of Isaac Pitman: Inventor of Phonography.* London: Griffith, Farran, Okeden and Welsh, 1890.

Regents of the Deseret University. "Minutes of the Board of Regents of the Deseret University." CHL, Salt Lake City, 1853.

———. The Book of Mormon, Part I. (𐐒 𐐀𐐶𐐬 𐐶𐐯 𐐌𐐬𐐻𐐲𐑉𐑋, 𐐓𐐩𐑉𐐻 I). Published for the Deseret University. New York: Russell Bros., 1869.

———. The Book of Mormon (𐐒 𐐀𐐶𐐬 𐐶𐐯 𐐌𐐬𐐻𐐲𐑉𐑋). Published for the Deseret University. New York: Russell Bros., 1869.

———. *The Deseret First Book.* Published for the Deseret University. New York: Russell Bros., 1868.

———. *The Deseret Second Book.* Published for the Deseret University. New York: Russell Bros., 1868.

Roberts, David. *The Pueblo Revolt: The Secret Rebellion that Drove the Spaniards Out of the Southwest*. New York: Simon & Schuster, 2004.

Rosenfelder, Mark. *The Language Construction Kit*. Chicago: Yonagu Books, 2010.

Sampson, Geoffrey. *Writing Systems*. London: Hutchinson, 1985.

Seaman, P. David, ed. "English-Hopi & Hopi-English Dictionary: by J. B. Epp and Other Mennonite Missionaries." Collated by P. David Seaman, August 1976. P. David Seaman Collection, box 7 fd 3, Special Collections and Archives, Cline Library, Northern Arizona University, Flagstaff, 1976.

———. *Hopi Dictionary*. Revised ed. Northern Arizona University Anthropological Paper 2. Flagstaff: Northern Arizona University, 1996.

Sekaquaptewa, Emory, and Barbara Pepper, eds. *Coyote & the Winnowing Birds: A Traditional Hopi Tale*. Santa Fe: Clear Light Publishers, 1994.

Shelton, Marion Jackson. "Diary 1858 March–1859 June." Marion Jackson Shelton Papers, MS 1412, fd 1, CHL, Salt Lake City, 1859.

———. *English-Hopi Vocabulary*. MS 2977. CHL, Salt Lake City, 1860.

———. Letter to Brigham Young, July 1859. Brigham Young Incoming Correspondence, CR 1234 1, reel 37, box 27, fd 5. CHL, Salt Lake City.

Shelton, Marion Jackson. Letter to Brigham Young, November 13, 1859. Brigham Young Incoming Correspondence, CR 1234 1, reel 37, box 27, fd 5. CHL, Salt Lake City.

———. Letter to Brigham Young, April 3, 1860. Brigham Young Incoming Correspondence, reel 38, box 27, fd 19. CHL, Salt Lake City.

———. Letter to Gentlemen, March 7, 1859. Marion Jackson Shelton Papers, MS 1412, fd 2. CHL, Salt Lake City.

———. Letter to George A. Smith, October 11, 1858. George A. Smith Incoming Correspondence. CHL, Salt Lake City.

———. Letter to George A. Smith, November 13, 1859. George A. Smith Incoming Correspondence. CHL, Salt Lake City.

———. Letter to George A. Smith, November 16, 1859. George A. Smith Incoming Correspondence, MS 1322, box 5, fd 19, item 10. CHL, Salt Lake City.

———. Letter to George A. Smith, Communication No. 3, January 22, 1859. George A. Smith Incoming Correspondence. CHL, Salt Lake City.

———. Letter to George L.[sic] Smith, R. Bentley, R. Campbell, J. J., J. V., and Others, November 13, 1859. George A. Smith Incoming Correspondence. CHL, Salt Lake City.

———. "Letter to the Editor." Correspondence. *Deseret News*, November 10, 1869, 476.

———. List of Words for Reference in the Deseret Letter Edition of the Book of Mormon. Probably late 1869. Deseret Alphabet Manuscripts, box 5, fd 1. CHL, Salt Lake City.

Simpson, James H. *Navaho Expedition: Journal of a Military Reconnaissance from Santa Fe, New Mexico, to the Navaho Country, Made in 1849 by Lieutenant James H. Simpson.* Edited by Frank McNitt. American Exploration and Travel Series. Norman: University of Oklahoma Press, 1964.

Smart, William B., and Donna T. Smart. *Over the Rim.* Logan: Utah State University Press, 1999.

Smith, Albert E. "Thales Hastings Haskell: Pioneer, Scout, Explorer, Indian Missionary." Typescript, L. Tom Perry Special Collections, Harold B. Lee Library, Brigham Young University, Provo, UT, 1964.

Snydergaard, Iris B. "Village of My Red Brother." *Frontier Times* 47, no. 4 (June–July 1973): 14–16, 51–53.

Steele, John. Letter to George A. Smith, January 8, 1863. Journal History. CHL, Salt Lake City.

———. "Map 1863." CHL, Salt Lake City, 1963.

Stout, Hosea. *Journal of Hosea Stout.* Edited by Juanita Brooks, 2 vols. Salt Lake City: University of Utah Press, 1964.

Titiev, Mischa. *Old Oraibi: A Study of the Hopi Indians of Third Mesa.* First published in 1944 as Papers of the Peabody Museum of American Archaeology and Ethnology 22, no. 1, Harvard University, Cambridge, MA. Albuquerque: University of New Mexico Press, 1992.

Turley, Richard E., Jr, ed. *Selected Collections from the Archives of the Church of Jesus Christ of Latter-day Saints.* 2 vols. 74 DVDs. Provo, UT: Brigham Young University Press, 2002.

Tyler, Guy, ed. Field audio recordings of Mrs. Monongya and Ruben Dawahoya, 1964. The Guy Tyler collection of Hopi sound recordings, LA 222.1, Berkeley Language Center, UC Berkeley.

Vocabulary of the Zuni Language. MS 6065, fds 1–2. CHL, Salt Lake City.

Voth, H. R. *Hopi Proper Names.* Anthropological Series 6, no. 3. Chicago: Field Columbian Museum, 1905.

———. "Hopi-English Vocabulary." Unpublished manuscript. Mennonite Library and Archives, Bethel College, New Newton, KS, 1902.

Walker, Ronald W., Richard E. Turley Jr., and Glen M. Leonard. *Massacre at Mountain Meadows.* Oxford: Oxford University Press, 2008.

Watt, George D. Letter to Willard Richards, February 5, 1848. Typescript, Chronology of George D. Watt. CHL, Salt Lake City.

Watt, Ronald G. "English Convert Used Phonography Skills in Development of Original Deseret Alphabet." *Pioneer* 30, no. 5 (September-October 1983): 8–9.

———. *The Mormon Passage of George D. Watt: First British Convert, Scribe for Zion.* Logan: Utah State University Press, 2009.

Whiteley, Peter M. "Bartering Pahos with the President." *Ethnohistory* 51, no. 2 (Spring 2004): 359–414.

———. *Deliberate Acts: Changing Hopi Culture through the Oraibi Split.* Tucson: University of Arizona Press, 1988.

————. *Rethinking Hopi Ethnography*. Washington, DC: Smithsonian Institution Press, 1998.

————. *The Oraibi Split: A Hopi Transformation*. Anthropological Papers of the American Museum of Natural History 87. New York: American Museum of Natural History, 2008.

Whiting, Alfred F. *You Can Record Hopi*. Photocopy in P. David Seaman Collection, box 1, fd 3, p. 595, Cline Library. Northern Arizona University, Flagstaff, 1969.

Whorf, Benjamin Lee. "The Hopi Language, Toreva Dialect." In *Linguistic Structures of Native America*, edited by Harry Hoijer, M. R. Haas, et al., 158–83. Viking Fund Publications in Anthropology 6. New York: Viking Fund, 1946.

Wilkinson, Charles. *Fire on the Plateau: Conflict and Endurance in the American Southwest*. Washington, DC: Island Press, 1999.

Wixom, Hartt. *Hamblin: A Modern Look at the Frontier Life and Legend of Jacob Hamblin*. Springville, UT: Cedar Fort, 1996.

Young, Brigham. Letter to George D. Watt, April 16, 1847. Watt Papers. CHL, Salt Lake City.

————. Letter to Jacob Hamblin, September 18, 1859. Brigham Young Outgoing Correspondence. CHL, Salt Lake City.